23 Ready-To-Go Lesson Plans
MATH
GRADE 1

www.themailbox.com

What Are Lifesaver Lessons®?

Lifesaver Lessons® are well-planned, easy-to-implement, curriculum-based lessons. Each lesson contains a complete materials list, step-by-step instructions, a reproducible activity or pattern, and several extension activities.

How Do I Use A Lifesaver Lesson?

Each Lifesaver Lesson is designed to decrease your preparation time and increase the amount of quality teaching time with your students. These lessons are great for introducing or reinforcing new concepts. You may want to look through the lessons to see what types of materials to gather. After completing a lesson, be sure to check out the fun-filled extension activities.

What Materials Will I Need?

Most of the materials for each lesson can be easily found in your classroom or school. Check the list of materials below for any items you may need to gather or purchase.

- crayons
- pencils
- scissors
- glue
- tape and tape dispenser
- rulers
- construction paper
- drawing paper
- chart paper
- bulletin-board paper
- poster board
- blank transparencies
- transparency markers

- overhead projector
- counters and other manipulatives
- large and small paper clips
- base ten rods and cubes
- world map
- small paper bag
- a real penny, nickel, and dime
- stapler
- notepad
- containers
- index cards

D1611883

Lifesaver Lessons®

Project Editor:
Sharon Murphy

Editor:
Susan Hohbach Walker

Writers:
Lisa Buchholz, Cynthia Holcomb, Lisa Kelly,
Juanita L. Krueger, Pamela Kucks, Sharon Murphy,
Sandra Shaw, Susan Hohbach Walker

Artists:
Cathy Spangler Bruce, Sheila Krill,
Rob Mayworth, Donna K. Teal

Cover Artist:
Jennifer Tipton Bennett

Table Of Contents

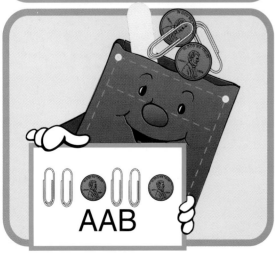

©1997 by THE EDUCATION CENTER, INC.
All rights reserved.
ISBN #1-56234-178-2

Except as provided for herein, no part of this publication may be reproduced or transmitted in any form or by any means, electronic or mechanical, including photocopying, recording, or storing in any information storage and retrieval system or electronic online bulletin board, without prior written permission from The Education Center, Inc. Permission is given to the original purchaser to reproduce patterns and reproducibles for individual classroom use only and not for resale or distribution. Reproduction for an entire school or school system is prohibited. Please direct written inquiries to The Education Center, Inc., P.O. Box 9753, Greensboro, NC 27429-0753. The Education Center®, *The Mailbox*®, Lifesaver Lessons®, and the mailbox/post/grass logo are registered trademarks of The Education Center, Inc. All other brand or product names are trademarks or registered trademarks of their respective companies.

Manufactured in the United States
10 9 8 7 6 5 4 3 2

The "Bear" Facts

Get down to the facts—addition facts, that is—with this honey of a lesson!

Skill: Determining addition facts to 6

Estimated Lesson Time: 30 minutes

Teacher Preparation:
1. Duplicate page 5 for each student.
2. Duplicate and cut out three copies of the unprogrammed bear pattern on page 6 on light brown construction paper.
3. Draw a large addition sign on a piece of drawing paper.

Materials:
1 copy of page 5 for each student
6 counters per student
1 piece of drawing paper labeled with an addition sign
3 light brown bear cutouts

Teacher Reference:
(Use with Step #2 on page 4.)

0 + 0 = 0	3 + 0 = 3	5 + 0 = 5	6 + 0 = 6
	0 + 3 = 3	0 + 5 = 5	0 + 6 = 6
1 + 0 = 1	2 + 1 = 3	1 + 4 = 5	1 + 5 = 6
0 + 1 = 1	1 + 2 = 3	4 + 1 = 5	5 + 1 = 6
		3 + 2 = 5	2 + 4 = 6
2 + 0 = 2	4 + 0 = 4	2 + 3 = 5	4 + 2 = 6
0 + 2 = 2	0 + 4 = 4		3 + 3 = 6
1 + 1 = 2	2 + 2 = 4		
	1 + 3 = 4		
	3 + 1 = 4		

ADDITION FACTS TO 6

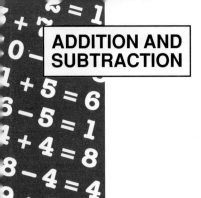

Introducing The Lesson:

Show students the three bear cutouts and the addition sign. Tell students that the bears will help them with today's math lesson.

Steps:

1. Ask for three student volunteers. Have one student hold one bear, one student hold nothing, and one student hold the addition sign and stand between the other two students. Read the addition sentence that the students have formed (1 + 0 = 1). Then have the students on opposite sides of the addition sign exchange places. Read the new addition sentence (0 + 1 = 1).

2. Repeat this activity in the same manner, using a total of two bears and then a total of three bears. See page 3 for the possible addition combinations for these sums.

3. Distribute a copy of page 5 and six counters to each student. Explain to students how to manipulate the counters on the bear's pots to make the sums shown.

4. Challenge students to complete the Bonus Box activity.

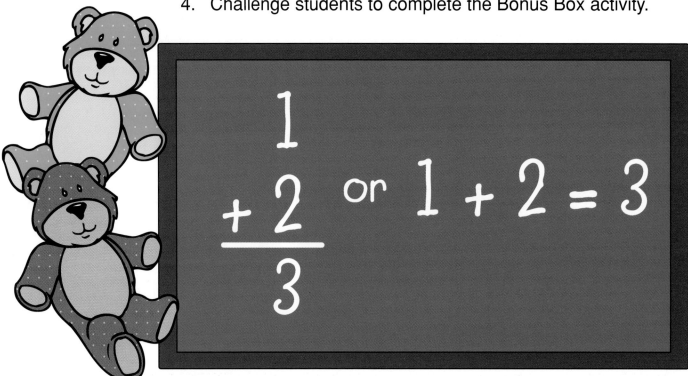

$$\begin{array}{r} 1 \\ + 2 \\ \hline 3 \end{array} \quad \text{or} \quad 1 + 2 = 3$$

Name_____

The "Bear" Facts

Find ways to make each sum.
Use counters.

Bonus Box: Write all the ways to make the sum 3 on the back of your paper.

_____ + _____ = 4   _____ + _____ = 4

_____ + _____ = 4   _____ + _____ = 4

_____ + _____ = 4

_____ + _____ = 5   _____ + _____ = 5

_____ + _____ = 5   _____ + _____ = 5

_____ + _____ = 5   _____ + _____ = 5

_____ + _____ = 6   _____ + _____ = 6

_____ + _____ = 6   _____ + _____ = 6

_____ + _____ = 6   _____ + _____ = 6

_____ + _____ = 6

©1997 The Education Center, Inc. • *Lifesaver Lessons*™ • Grade 1 • TEC503

How To Extend The Lesson:

- Use disposable dinner plates (divided into one large and two small sections) for practicing addition. Each child needs one plate and a supply of counters. Have the child place a few counters into each small section; then find the sum of the sets by grouping the counters together in the large section.

5	1
4	0
2	3

- There's no doubt students will enjoy this small-group game. Use chalk to draw a game mat (similar to the one shown) on the pavement outside. The first player tosses two beanbags and announces the sum of the numbers on which the bags land. The other players follow in the same manner. The player with the greatest sum wins the round.

- Create bear flash cards. Enlarge and duplicate a supply of the unprogrammed bear pattern below on light brown construction paper. Cut out the bears and write a different math fact on each bear. Laminate the bears for durability. A small group of students may use the flash cards to test one another. Or use the bears as a warm-up activity to test the class.

- Duplicate copies of the programmed bear badge below for your students.

I'm "beary" good at addition!

©1997 The Education Center, Inc. • *Lifesaver Lessons*™ • Grade 1 • TEC503

Determining addition facts to 6

Bubble-Gum Addition

*Goody! Goody! Gumball! Students' addition skills are sure to stick
with this tasty activity!*

Skill: Solving addition facts to 12

Estimated Lesson Time: 40 minutes

Teacher Preparation:
1. Draw a gumball machine on the board.
2. Cut a class supply of construction-paper circles to use as gumballs for the machine.
3. Duplicate page 9 for each student.

Materials:
5 gumballs, gumball cutouts, or other small
   manipulatives
1 copy of page 9 per student
12 manipulatives per student pair
supply of construction-paper circles that
   resemble gumballs
1 paper clip per student
tape
1 pencil per student

Teacher Reference:
Addition vocabulary:
- Two *plus* one equals three.
- The *sum* of two and one is three.
- The *total* of two and one is three.
- If two and one are added together, there are three *in all.*

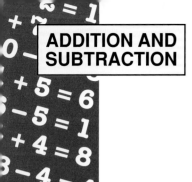

Introducing The Lesson:

Place three gumballs, gumball cutouts, or other small manipulatives in a student's hand. Tell the class how many gumballs that student is holding. Then place two gumballs in another student's hand. Tell the class this amount also. Ask a volunteer to tell the class how to find the total number of gumballs in the students' hands. Write the corresponding addition problem on the chalkboard.

Steps:

1. Pair students and distribute 12 manipulatives to each student pair.

2. Announce an addition problem (with a sum to 12) and have each student pair use the manipulatives to solve the problem. Call on a volunteer to answer the problem. If the answer is correct, have the student tape a gumball cutout inside the machine drawn on the board. Repeat the activity until all student pairs have provided an answer.

3. Distribute a copy of page 9 and a paper clip to each student.

4. Demonstrate to students how to use a paper clip and a pencil to create a spinner on the gumball machine as shown below.

5. Challenge students to complete the Bonus Box activity.

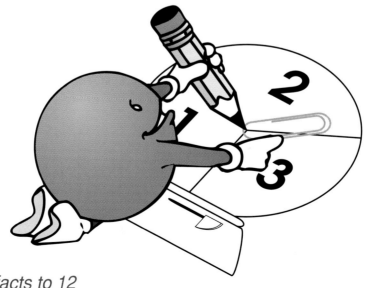

Bubble-Gum Addition

Use a pencil and a paper clip to make a spinner.
Spin the paper clip.
Write the number in the box.
Add.
Write the answer in the gumball.

1. 9 + ☐ = ◯

2. 0 + ☐ = ◯

3. 4 + ☐ = ◯

4. 8 + ☐ = ◯

5. 3 + ☐ = ◯

6. 2 + ☐ = ◯

7. 1 + ☐ = ◯

8. 6 + ☐ = ◯

9. 7 + ☐ = ◯

10. 5 + ☐ = ◯

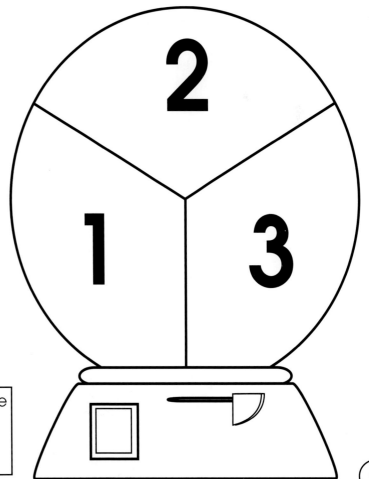

Bonus Box: Use the spinner to spin five more addition problems. Write them on a piece of paper. Give them to a classmate to solve.

©1997 The Education Center, Inc. • *Lifesaver Lessons*™ • Grade 1 • TEC503

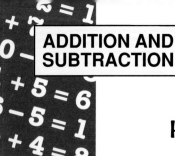
How To Extend The Lesson:

- Draw six gumball-machine shapes on the board and number them from one to six. Call out addition problems and have each student work the problems on scrap paper. For each problem, call on a student to draw a gumball on the machine numbered with the correct sum.

- Have students dictate story problems about gumballs. Record the story problems on chart paper. Distribute manipulatives and have students solve the problems as you read each problem aloud to the class.

- Distribute a small strip of paper labeled with an addition problem to each student. Have him glue the strip to the back of a piece of drawing paper and then draw a picture illustrating the addition fact on the front side. Display the completed pictures for students to determine the equations used.

- Enlarge, color, and cut out a class supply of the gumball-machine pattern shown below. Use clear Con-Tact® paper to attach the cut-out to each student's desk. When a student hands in a math homework assignment, apply a sticker to the machine. Use this record-keeping method to keep track of each student's assignments; then provide a reward when the machine is full.

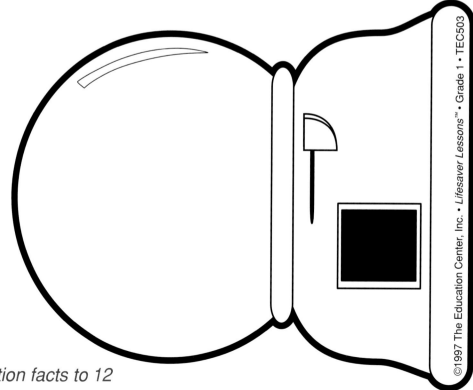

©1997 The Education Center, Inc. • *Lifesaver Lessons*™ • Grade 1 • TEC503

A Patch Of Watermelon Facts

Sweeten your students' subtraction skills with this mouthwatering lesson!

Skill: Creating and solving subtraction facts to six

Estimated Lesson Time: 30 minutes

Teacher Preparation:

1. Duplicate page 13 for each student.
2. Obtain or make a set of subtraction flash cards featuring the subtraction facts listed in the Teacher Reference below.
3. Draw two watermelons, without seeds, on the chalkboard. Label one watermelon "Team 1" and the other "Team 2."

Materials:
1 copy of page 13 per student
a set of subtraction flash cards
scissors

Teacher Reference:

6 − 6 = 0	5 − 5 = 0	3 − 3 = 0
6 − 5 = 1	5 − 4 = 1	3 − 2 = 1
6 − 4 = 2	5 − 3 = 2	3 − 1 = 2
6 − 3 = 3	5 − 2 = 3	3 − 0 = 3
6 − 2 = 4	5 − 1 = 4	
6 − 1 = 5	5 − 0 = 5	2 − 2 = 0
6 − 0 = 6		2 − 1 = 1
	4 − 4 = 0	2 − 0 = 2
	4 − 3 = 1	
	4 − 2 = 2	1 − 1 = 0
	4 − 1 = 3	1 − 0 = 1
	4 − 0 = 4	
		0 − 0 = 0

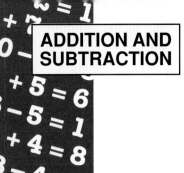

Introducing The Lesson:

Tell students that they are going to work in teams to answer subtraction problems. The team whose watermelon has the most seeds at the end of the game wins.

Steps:

1. Divide students into two teams. Name one team, Team 1, and the other team, Team 2. Have team members sit together.

2. Show a student from Team 1 a subtraction flash card. Have her announce the answer. If the answer is correct, draw a seed on Team 1's watermelon. If the answer is incorrect, ask a student from Team 2 to solve the problem. If he is correct, award a watermelon seed to Team 2. If he is incorrect, continue alternating between the two teams until a student correctly solves the problem.

3. Continue displaying flash cards to the two teams (in this alternating fashion) until all students have had a turn. The team with the most watermelon seeds wins.

4. Distribute a copy of page 13 to each student.

5. Explain the directions on the reproducible to your students as follows:
    *   Cut out the seeds and place them facedown on your desk.
    *   Choose two seeds. Use them to write a subtraction problem; then solve the problem. (Remember: The largest number is always first. For example, 6 – 3 = 3 is a possible problem but 3 – 6 is not because six cannot be taken away from three.)
    *   Return the two seeds facedown on your desk.
    *   Continue in this same manner, writing a different subtraction problem each time.

A Patch Of Watermelon Facts

Cut out the seeds.
Place them facedown.
Draw two seeds.
Make a subtraction problem.
Write.
Solve.

☐ – ☐ = _____   ☐ – ☐ = _____

☐ – ☐ = _____   ☐ – ☐ = _____

☐ – ☐ = _____   ☐ – ☐ = _____

☐ – ☐ = _____   ☐ – ☐ = _____

☐ – ☐ = _____   ☐ – ☐ = _____

☐ – ☐ = _____   ☐ – ☐ = _____

☐ – ☐ = _____   ☐ – ☐ = _____

©1997 The Education Center, Inc. • *Lifesaver Lessons*™ • Grade 1 • TEC503

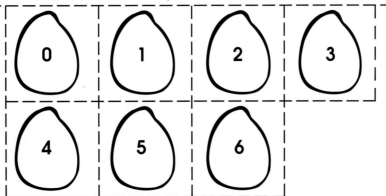

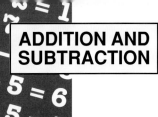

How To Extend The Lesson:

- Engage students in subtraction practice by rolling dice. Divide students into small groups and provide a pair of dice for each group. Instruct students in each group to take turns rolling the dice, forming a subtraction problem with the numbers rolled, and then solving the problem.

- For a tasty math activity, serve each child a slice of watermelon. Have students save their seeds, clean them, and then use them as manipulatives to solve subtraction problems.

- Whet students' appetites for subtraction with subtraction word problems featuring watermelons. Ask students to solve problems, such as "If Jamie has six watermelons and she gives two watermelons to her friend Katherine, how many watermelons does Jamie have left?" Students will enjoy solving similar problems and creating their own.

- Have students write subtraction problems using dominos. Provide each child with a domino and a recording sheet similar to the one shown. Instruct the child to illustrate the face of his domino in the space provided on the recording sheet, and then use the domino to write two subtraction sentences. After the student has completed his domino subtraction problems, have him exchange dominos with a classmate and repeat the activity. Have students continue in this manner until completing the reproducible.

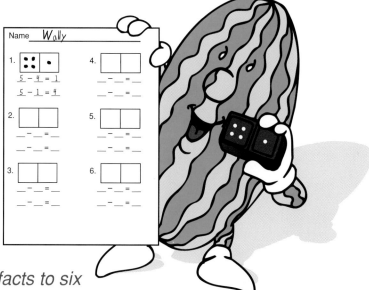

Creating and solving subtraction facts to six

Totally Turtle

Your youngsters are sure to come out of their shells for this subtraction lesson!

Skill: Solving subtraction facts to 12

Estimated Lesson Time: 30 minutes

Teacher Preparation:

1. Use the pattern on page 16 to duplicate a class supply of turtles.
2. Duplicate page 17 for each student.

Materials:

1 turtle pattern (page 16) per student
1 copy of page 17 per student
crayons

Teacher Reference:

Subtraction vocabulary:
• Five *minus* three equals two.
• Five *take away* two equals three.
• The *difference* between five and three is two.
• If three is subtracted from five, two *remains.*
• If three is subtracted from five, two is *left.*

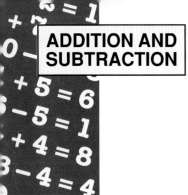

Introducing The Lesson:

Distribute a turtle strip to each student. Instruct each child to write a subtraction problem on the front of it and write the answer and her name on the back. Be sure to set a limit on the highest numeral students may use.

Steps:

1. Review with your students basic subtraction strategies, such as subtracting zero from a number and subtracting the number from itself.

2. Have each child exchange turtles with a classmate. Using scrap paper, have the student solve the problem on her classmate's turtle, then turn the turtle over to see if her answer is correct. After checking her answer, have her exchange that turtle for another student's turtle, solve the new subtraction problem, and check her answer.

3. Have students continue to exchange turtles in the same manner for approximately ten minutes.

4. Distribute page 17 to each student.

5. Challenge each child to complete the Bonus Box activity.

©1997 The Education Center, Inc. • *Lifesaver Lessons*™ • Grade 1 • TEC503

Name _____

Totally Turtle

Subtract.
Color by the code.

0, 1, and 2—**yellow**
3, 4, and 5—**blue**
6 and 7—**red**
8 and 9—**orange**
10 and 11—**purple**

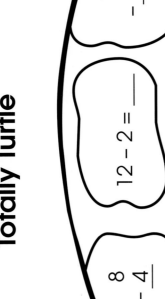

$8 - 2 =$ ___

$12 - 1 =$ ___

$9 - 2 =$ ___

$7 - 6 =$ ___

$\begin{array}{r} 11 \\ -\ 2 \\ \hline \end{array}$

$12 - 2 =$ ___

$5 - 5 =$ ___

$7 - 2 =$ ___

$9 - 1 =$ ___

$6 - 4 =$ ___

$\begin{array}{r} 8 \\ -\ 4 \\ \hline \end{array}$

$10 - 3 =$ ___

$10 - 1 =$ ___

$11 - 0 =$ ___

$4 - 1 =$ ___

Bonus Box: Make your own turtle shell of subtraction problems and give it to a classmate to solve.

©1997 The Education Center, Inc. • Lifesaver Lessons™ • Grade 1 • TEC503

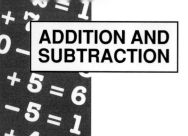

How To Extend The Lesson:

- Have students use calculators to check the answers to the problems on page 17.

- Divide students into small groups and supply each group with a paper bag and 12 counters. Have one child in each group place the counters in the bag. Then call on another child in each group to take out a specific number of counters. Ask those students, "How many counters are still in the bag?" Have the children in each group empty the bag to verify the answer. Continue the activity by calling out a different number of counters to take out.

- Duplicate copies of the turtle strip on page 16 to make subtraction flash cards. Students can use the cards to quiz themselves or each other.

- For this small-group subtraction game, remove the face cards and aces from a deck of playing cards; then stack the remaining cards facedown on a playing surface. To play, the first of four players selects two playing cards from the pile, turns them over, and subtracts the lower number printed on the cards from the higher number. He announces his answer to the group and the other players verify his calculations. To complete the round, the remaining players repeat this process. At the end of the round, students determine which player had the lowest difference. Play continues for as many rounds as desired.

7 − 5 = 2

Tic-Fact-Toe

It's a fact! Your youngsters will enjoy practicing addition and subtraction facts with this one-of-a-kind math lesson!

Skill: Determining and solving addition and subtraction facts to 12

Estimated Lesson Time: 30 minutes

Teacher Preparation:

1. Duplicate page 21 for each student pair.
2. Draw a large tic-tac-toe grid on the chalkboard. Program each square with a different addition or subtraction problem.

Materials:

1 copy of page 21 per student pair

Quick Tip: Remember to model both horizontal and vertical notation with addition and subtraction problems.

$$2 + 1 = 3$$

$$\begin{array}{r} 2 \\ + 1 \\ \hline 3 \end{array}$$

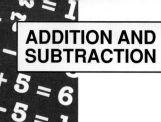
Introducing The Lesson:

Challenge your students to a game of Tic-Fact-Toe. Divide the class into two teams. Assign one group to be the Xs and one group to be the Os. Call on one student from team X to choose a box and solve the problem. Check the answer. If the answer is correct, have her put an X in that box on the chalkboard. If her answer is incorrect, choose a student from team O to solve the problem. Continue in this manner, alternating between both teams, until one team has tic-fact-toe.

Steps:

1. Distribute a copy of page 21 to each student pair. To begin play, have each pair decide who will be X and O. The X player begins Game 1 by choosing a problem to solve. Then he writes the answer under the problem and puts an X in the box. Next the O player chooses a problem and repeats the same process using an O. Each twosome continues to alter-nate play until one person scores tic-fact-toe or until all the squares have been marked.

2. The children then play another game of Tic-Fact-Toe using Game 2. The O player begins Game 2.

Names: _____

_____ is X.   _____ is O.

Tic-Fact-Toe

In turn, solve a problem.
Write X or O in the box.
Try to get three in a row.

Game 1

$\begin{array}{r} 10 \\ -\ 7 \\ \hline \end{array}$	$\begin{array}{r} 6 \\ +\ 3 \\ \hline \end{array}$	$\begin{array}{r} 4 \\ -\ 4 \\ \hline \end{array}$
$\begin{array}{r} 1 \\ +\ 9 \\ \hline \end{array}$	$\begin{array}{r} 8 \\ -\ 3 \\ \hline \end{array}$	$\begin{array}{r} 2 \\ +\ 6 \\ \hline \end{array}$
$\begin{array}{r} 5 \\ +\ 7 \\ \hline \end{array}$	$\begin{array}{r} 11 \\ -\ 4 \\ \hline \end{array}$	$\begin{array}{r} 12 \\ -\ 6 \\ \hline \end{array}$

Game 2

$10 - 6 =$ ___	$7 + 2 =$ ___	$9 - 4 =$ ___
$5 + 5 =$ ___	$1 + 11 =$ ___	$12 - 12 =$ ___
$0 + 3 =$ ___	$6 - 5 =$ ___	$2 + 8 =$ ___

©1997 The Education Center, Inc. • Lifesaver Lessons™ • Grade 1 • TEC503

How To Extend The Lesson:

- Duplicate a copy of page 21 and white-out the problems; then reprogram the reproducible with different addition and subtraction problems. Students will enjoy playing Tic-Fact-Toe over and over again!

- This five-minute filler is sure to be a class favorite! Whenever there is an idle moment, announce a Number For The Day. Have each student write the number on a piece of paper, then quickly write math facts that equal that number on his paper. If desired reward the student who lists the most correct facts in the allotted time.

- Have each student create his own worksheet of addition and subtraction problems. After creating an answer key for his worksheet, have the student exchange papers with a fellow classmate.

- Try this twist to the usual flash-card drill when practicing basic addition or subtraction facts. Divide students into two or more groups and have them number off from 0 to 12 in each group. Each time a flash card is displayed, have only the students whose number equals the sum or difference of the card respond.

- Duplicate copies of the award below for students.

IT'S A FACT!

_____
(student)

can add and subtract!

Teacher: _____

Date: _____

©1997 The Education Center, Inc.

Place Value In A Pocket

Get your students hopping into place value with this hands-on activity.

Skill: Determining place value to 49

Estimated Lesson Time: 30 minutes

Teacher Preparation:
1. Duplicate page 25 for each student.
2. Provide base ten blocks (4 rods and 9 cubes) per student.

Materials:
1 copy of page 25 per student
4 base ten rods and 9 base ten cubes per student (can substitute craft sticks and beans)
scissors
world map
  (optional)

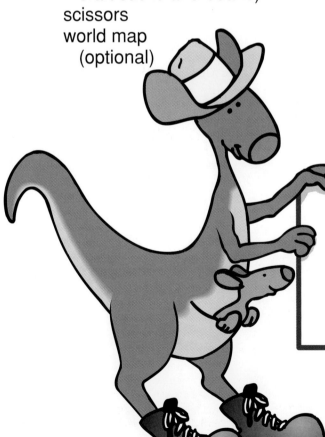

Quick Tip: To help students remember that the tens are on the left and the ones are on the right, have them write "TO" above the numeral and then draw a line down the middle.

T	O
3	4

Introducing The Lesson:

Tell your students to fasten their seat belts because they are taking a flight to Australia. (Use the world map to show students the location of Australia.) While en route tell your students that they are traveling to Australia to get something they need for their math lesson—kangaroos!

Steps:

1. Distribute a copy of page 25 to each student.

2. Have each student cut out the numeral cards on the side of his reproducible.

3. Distribute four base ten rods and nine base ten cubes to each student.

4. Call out a number from 1 to 49. Have each student place the correct tens numeral card and ones numeral card on the appropriate kangaroos' hats. Then have each student use the base ten rods and cubes to show the announced number on the kangaroos' pouches.

5. Have students clear the rods, cubes, and cards off their kangaroos. Then repeat the activity several times by calling out different numbers.

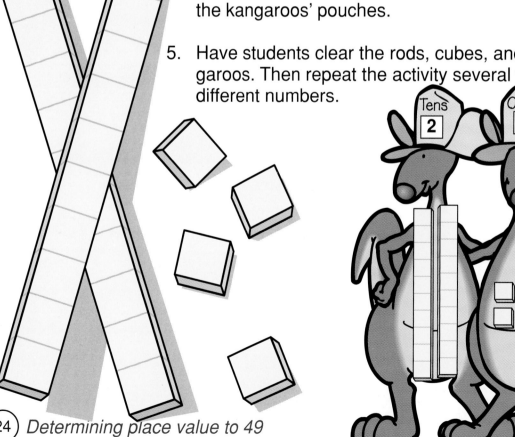

Determining place value to 49

Place Value In A Pocket

1
2
3
4
5
6
7
8
9
0
1
2
3
4

©1997 The Education Center, Inc. • *Lifesaver Lessons*™ • Grade 1 • TEC503

25

How To Extend The Lesson:

- Have students line up along a starting line. Call out a number of tens and a number of ones (such as "One ten and two ones"). Students determine the number and hop that number of times toward a finish line. Continue the activity until the class reaches the designated finish line.

- Give each student one minute to draw as many triangles as possible. Have each student circle groups of ten, count the groups, and then count the ones to determine the number of triangles he drew.

- Use Unifix® cubes to determine how many items of blue clothing are being worn in your class. Distribute a cube for each item of blue clothing a student is wearing. Then have students work in groups to put their cubes together in groups of ten. Next collect all the cubes, combining leftover cubes in groups of ten whenever possible. Count groups of tens and ones cubes to determine the number of blue items being worn by your class. Repeat the activity using a different color.

- This partner game provides plenty of place-value practice. Each pair of students will need two place-value mats similar to the one shown, a die, and a set of base ten rods and cubes. To play the game, each player in turn rolls the die and places that number of cubes in the ones column on his place-value mat. When a player has ten cubes in the ones column, he exchanges them for one rod and places it in the tens column. The first player to collect five tens wins!

Tens	Ones

Pigging Out On Place Value

Your students are sure to have a "swine" time with this place-value lesson.

Skill: Determining place value to 99

Estimated Lesson Time: 30 minutes

Teacher Preparation:
1. Duplicate page 29 for each student.
2. Duplicate a class supply of pig patterns (page 30) onto pink construction paper.
3. Cut out each pig pattern. Write a different numeral from 1 to 99 on each pig.
4. Choose 16 numbers from 1–99. Write each of these numerals on a different slip of paper.

Materials:
1 copy of page 29 per student
1 pig (labeled with a numeral) per student
a large supply of base ten rods and cubes
   (optional: see "Quick Tip" below)
16 slips of paper, each labeled with a different numeral
bingo markers or other appropriate markers
scissors
marker
glue

Quick Tip:
Listed below are a variety of inexpensive materials that can be used to represent tens and ones (in place of base ten rods and cubes):
- dried beans and tongue depressors, cups, or lids
- macaroni and tongue depressors, cups, or lids
- buttons and tongue depressors, cups, or lids
- stickers and tongue depressors
- paper clips
- computer paper edges with holes
- Cheerios® and licorice sticks

Introducing The Lesson:

Distribute a pig cutout and a supply of base ten rods and cubes to each student. Have each student use his rods and cubes to show the number on his pig. Move around the classroom to check students' work. Then provide a signal, such as an oink, for each student to exchange his pig with a classmate's pig and repeat the activity. Have students continue in this same manner for approximately five minutes.

Steps:

1. Ask each student to share the number on his last pig and the value of the number (for example, "56 is five tens and six ones").

2. Ask students to respond to statements about their pigs such as "Oink if your pig's number is greater than 80," or "Oink if your pig's number is less than 45." (See below for additional ideas.)

3. Distribute a copy of page 29 and a supply of bingo markers to each student.

4. Read the 16 numbers (from the slips of paper) to students as they write them in the squares at the bottom of the page. Then instruct students to cut out the squares and randomly glue each one in a different box at the top of the page.

5. To play the game Oink, draw a numbered slip of paper and announce the value of the number on the paper. (For example, if the number is 73, announce, "Seven tens and three ones.") The students determine the number, search for it on their gameboards, and use a marker to cover it up. The first player to have four numbers covered in a row says, "Oink!" To claim the win, the player must read each number on his gameboard and state its value.

Oink if the number on your pig:

- is less than 50
- is greater than 25
- has a six in the ones place
- has an eight in the tens place
- has an even number in the ones place
- has an odd number in the tens place

Name_____

Oink!

Listen and write.
Cut. Glue.
Listen and play.

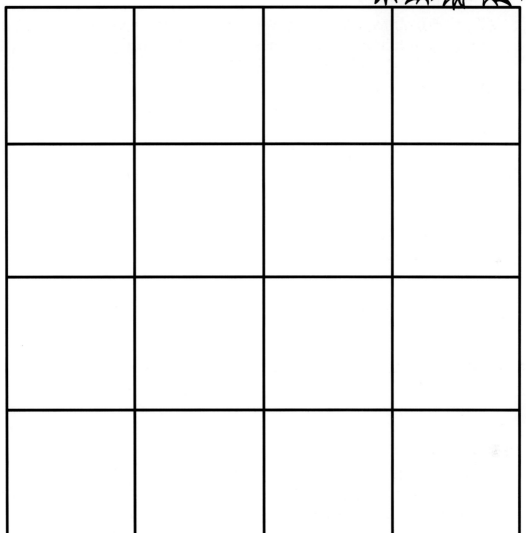

©1997 The Education Center, Inc. • *Lifesaver Lessons™* • Grade 1 • TEC503

How To Extend The Lesson:

- Repeat the activity on page 29 using different numbers.

- Provide students with three single-digit numerals (such as 1, 2, and 3) and ask them to determine all the two-digit numerals they can make with only those numerals *(11, 22, 33, 12, 13, 21, 23, 31, 32).*

- Challenge students to play a new variety of 20 Questions that features numbers. To begin the game, choose a number from 0 to 99. Students then have to ask you questions about the number that can be answered with a yes or a no. Instruct students to ask questions relating to the value of the number's digits, such as "Does the number have a four in the ones place?" or "Does the number have a three in the tens place?" Encourage students to guess the number in 20 questions or less.

Pattern

- Supply students with newspapers. Have each student cut out several two-digit numerals from a newspaper and glue them to a piece of paper. Then have students write the correct number of tens and ones beside each numeral.

- Use the pig pattern to create awards for your students. To make an award, duplicate a copy of the pig pattern; then write "[Student's name] has gone hog-wild over place value!" Sign your name and the date; then present the award to the deserving student.

©1997 The Education Center, Inc. • *Lifesaver Lessons*™ • Grade 1 • TEC503

Hopping Down The Number Trail

Now "hare" this! This math lesson will get your students hopping to sequence numbers to 100!

Skills: Sequencing numbers to 100; using the concept of *before* and *after*

Estimated Lesson Time: 40 minutes

Teacher Preparation:

1. Draw a chart on the chalkboard similar to the one shown below. Leaving a blank square for each child to fill in, program the squares with numbers from 1 to 100.
2. Draw a rabbit and a carrot on the chalkboard as shown. (Or tape cutouts to the board, if desired.) Label the rabbit "Mr. Rabbit."
3. Duplicate page 33 for each student.
4. Duplicate the hundreds chart on page 91 for each pair of students.

Materials:

1 copy of page 33 per student
1 copy of page 91 per student pair
1 bunny and carrot drawn on or taped to the chalkboard

Mr. Rabbit

1	2		4	5	6	7	8		10
	12	13	14		16	17		19	
21		23	24	25		27	28	29	30
31	32	33		35	36	37	38		40
	42			45	46			49	
51	52	53	54		56	57		59	60
	62	63	64		66		68	69	70
71		73	74	75		77	78		80
81	82		84	85	86		88	89	
91	92	93		95		97	98	99	

Sequencing numbers to 100; using the concept of before *and* after

Introducing The Lesson:

Point to Mr. Rabbit on the chalkboard and introduce him to your students. Tell them that Mr. Rabbit needs their help to get to his carrot. Explain to them that their job is to fill in the missing numbers on the chart drawn on the chalkboard.

Steps:

1. Have students form a line near the chalkboard. Beginning with the first student in line, have him determine the first missing number, write it in the square, and then return to his seat. Continue in this manner until each student has had a turn.

2. After the chart is complete, have students orally count to 100.

3. Pair students and distribute a hundreds chart (page 91) to each student pair. Then distribute a copy of page 33 to each student.

4. Explain the following directions to your students:
    To play the game, Player One holds the hundreds chart so Player Two cannot see it and then announces a number aloud. Player Two writes the number in the middle square of problem one on his paper. He then writes the number that comes before it and the number that comes after it. After completing the problem, he gives his paper to Player One to check. Players then switch roles and Player Two holds the number chart and announces a number for Player One to use in completing his problem. Play continues in this same manner until each player has completed ten problems.

5. Challenge each student to complete the Bonus Box activity.

Name ___Matthew Taylor___   *Sequencing numbers to 100*

Hopping Down the Number Trail

Listen to the directions.
Play this game with a partner

1. | 45 | **46** | 47 | 6. ☐ ☐ ☐

2. | 22 | 23 | 24 | 7. ☐ ☐ ☐

Sequencing numbers to 100; using the concept of before *and* after

Name _____

Hopping Down The Number Trail

Listen to the directions.
Play this game with a partner.

Example: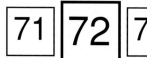

1.

2.

3.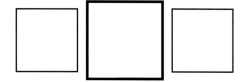

4.

5.

6.

7.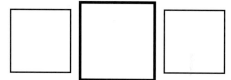

8.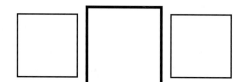

9.

10.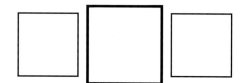

Bonus Box: On the back of this paper, write five numbers. Write the number that comes before each number and the number that comes after each number.

©1997 The Education Center, Inc. • Lifesaver Lessons™ • Grade 1 • TEC503

How To Extend The Lesson:

- Have students use hundreds charts to practice skip-counting. Give each child a copy of a hundreds chart and a supply of small manipulatives such as dried beans, buttons, or cubes. Have students use the manipulatives to cover the numbers as they skip-count by twos, fives, and then tens.

- This center activity provides students with practice counting to 100. Choose several small items—such as pennies, buttons, cubes, and counters—and place a different number of each in separate containers. Write the number of items in each container on an index card and place it facedown at the center. To begin the activity, a child chooses a container, counts the number of items in it, and then checks his answer on the answer card. He continues in the same manner until he has counted the objects in all the containers.

Pattern

- Share stories involving the number 100 with your students. *From One To One Hundred* by Teri Sloat (Dutton Children's Books, 1995) and *The 100th Day Of School* by Angela S. Medearis (Scholastic Inc., 1996) are both good choices.

- Duplicate several copies of the bunny pattern shown at the left on white construction paper. Program each pattern with a different number from 1 to 100. Laminate the cards; then place them at a center. Have students at the center work together to sequence the numbers on the cards.

©1997 The Education Center, Inc. • *Lifesaver Lessons*™ • Grade 1 • TEC503

Sequencing numbers to 100; using the concept of before *and* after

A Dinosaur Lineup!

This "dino-mite" activity will provide your youngsters some colossal practice with ordinal numbers!

Skill: Using ordinal numbers and ordinal number words

Estimated Lesson Time: 40 minutes

Teacher Preparation:

1. Duplicate the ten dinosaur patterns at the bottom of the page for each student.
2. Duplicate page 37 for each student.

Materials:

10 dinosaur patterns (below) per student
1 copy of page 37 per student
crayons
scissors

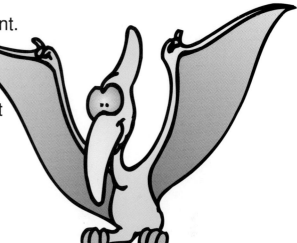

©1997 The Education Center, Inc. • *Lifesaver Lessons*™ • Grade 1 • TEC503

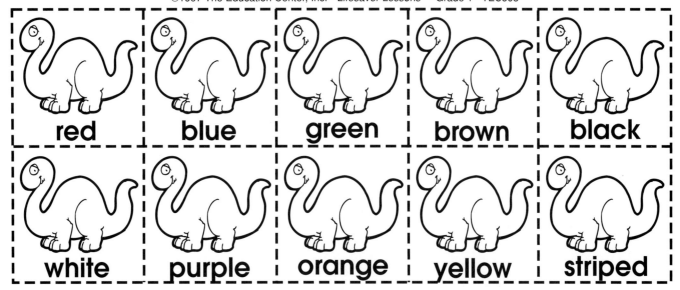

| red | blue | green | brown | black |
| white | purple | orange | yellow | striped |

Using ordinal numbers and ordinal number words (35)

Introducing The Lesson:

Line students up in three lines and give simple, oral directions for students to follow. Consider directions such as "If you are second in line, jump up and down," or "If you are sixth in line, put your hands on your head." Continue the activity until each person in line has had a chance to do a movement.

Steps:

1. Distribute one set of dinosaur patterns (page 35) to each student. Instruct each child to color each dinosaur the assigned color or pattern; then have her cut out the dinosaur cards.

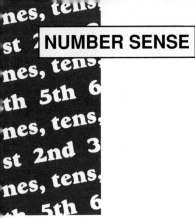

orange

first
1st

2. Provide students with a set of oral directions that direct them how to place the dinosaur cutouts in order (from left to right) on their desks. An example of such a set of directions might be, "The green dinosaur is first in line, the yellow dinosaur is second, the striped dinosaur is third,…"

3. Ask students to use their resulting dinosaur lineups to answer a variety of questions about ordinal numbers, such as "What color is the fourth dinosaur?"

green

second
2nd

4. Then distribute a copy of page 37 to each student. Have students listen to and follow these oral directions for coloring the reproducible:

   Row 1: Color the third dinosaur red, the ninth dinosaur green, the first dinosaur yellow, the eighth dinosaur brown, and the second dinosaur orange.

   Row 2: Color the tenth dinosaur blue, the fifth dinosaur black, the sixth dinosaur purple, the third dinosaur yellow, and the seventh dinosaur green.

   Row 3: Color the fourth dinosaur brown, the ninth dinosaur red, the fifth dinosaur orange, the first dinosaur purple, and the eighth dinosaur blue.

   Row 4: Use your pencil. Put an *X* on the eighth dinosaur, circle the first dinosaur, draw a hat on the tenth dinosaur, draw a line under the fifth dinosaur, and draw spots on the second dinosaur.

striped

third
3rd

5. Challenge each child to complete the Bonus Box activity.

Name _____

Dinosaur Lineups

Listen and do.

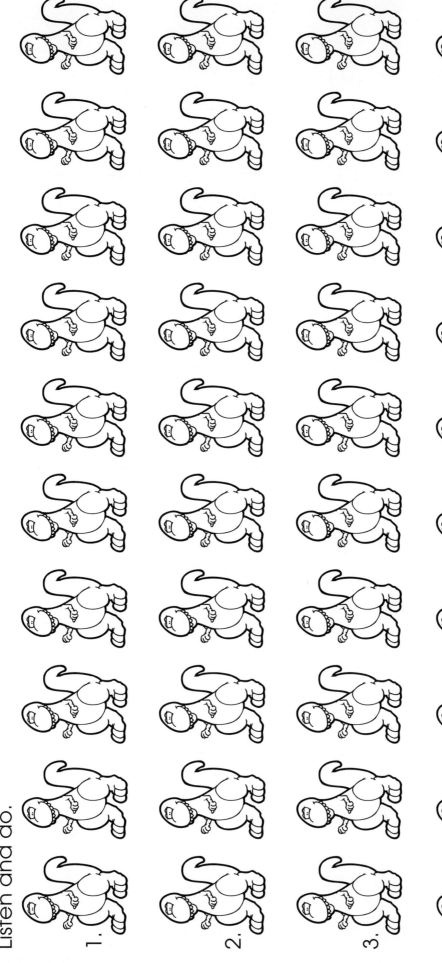

1.

2.

3.

4.

Bonus Box: Create a new kind of dinosaur. Draw a picture of it on the back of this sheet. Then write five sentences describing your dinosaur.

©1997 The Education Center, Inc. • *Lifesaver Lessons*™ • Grade 1 • TEC503

How To Extend The Lesson:

- Duplicate page 37 again and provide students with a new set of oral directions to complete the reproducible.

- Have students use ordinal number words to write a story describing what they did yesterday.

- Reinforce ordinal numbers with this small-group activity. Gather a paper-towel tube and five different-colored cubes. Hold the tube in a horizontal position and insert the cubes, one at a time, into one end of the tube. As each cube is inserted, use the appropriate ordinal number as you announce the color of the cube. (For example, the red cube is first.) Then have a student guess the order in which the cubes will spill out the other end of the tube. After recording the student's responses, gently tilt the tube so that the cubes spill out the other end—one at a time. Compare the student's guesses with the actual results. Repeat the activity several times, having a different student volunteer and a new color-cube sequence each time.

- Duplicate copies of the award shown below for your students. To reuse the award for another skill, simply white-out "ordinal numbers" and replace it with the new skill.

"DINO-MITE" WORK
This is to report that

_____
student

has done a "dino-mite" job with ordinal numbers!

_____
teacher signature

©1997 The Education Center, Inc. • Lifesaver Lessons™ • Grade 1 • TEC503

Using ordinal numbers and ordinal number words

What A Handful!

This hands-on math lesson will give your students plenty of estimation practice!

Skill: Estimating how many

Estimated Lesson Time: 30 minutes

Teacher Preparation:

1. Duplicate page 41 for each student.
2. For each student group (five students or less), fill separate wide-lid containers with five different items listed below in the Quick Tip. Place each set of five containers in a different area of the classroom.

Materials:

1 copy of page 41 per student
five containers of items for each student group

Quick Tip:

Suggested items for students to estimate: counters, Unifix® cubes, dried beans, checkers, marbles, toasted oat cereal, M&M's®, Q-tips®, cotton balls, pennies, miniature marshmallows, acorns, peanuts in the shell, bottle caps, sugar cubes, and paper clips

Introducing The Lesson:

Ask each student to hold up one hand. Tell students that they will be using their hands to complete their math lesson on estimation today. Explain to students that they are each going to *estimate,* or guess, how many items will fit in one of their hands.

Steps:

1. Distribute a copy of page 41 to each student.

2. Divide students into groups of five or less. Assign each student group to a different station in the classroom (where a set of containers has been set up).

3. Have each student write each of the five items at his station under the column on his paper labeled "Item ."

4. Then have each student choose an item at his station, estimate how many he would be able to hold in one hand, and then record his estimate in the space provided. Next have each child reach into the container and grab as many items as possible. The student uses tally marks to count the number of items in his hand, and then records the actual number of items in the appropriate location on the chart. Students continue in the same manner for the additional four items at the station.

5. Challenge each student to complete the Bonus Box activity.

Name __Breyanna Lynne__ _____ Estimation

Handy Estimation

Follow your teacher's directions.

	Item	Estimate	Tally Of Items	Actual number
1.	beans	50	ЖНН ЖНН ЖНН lll	18
2.	paper clips			
3.	marbles			
4.	checkers			
5.	unifix cubes			

Bonus Box: Which item had the best estimate? _____

Name _____

Handy Estimation

Follow your teacher's directions.

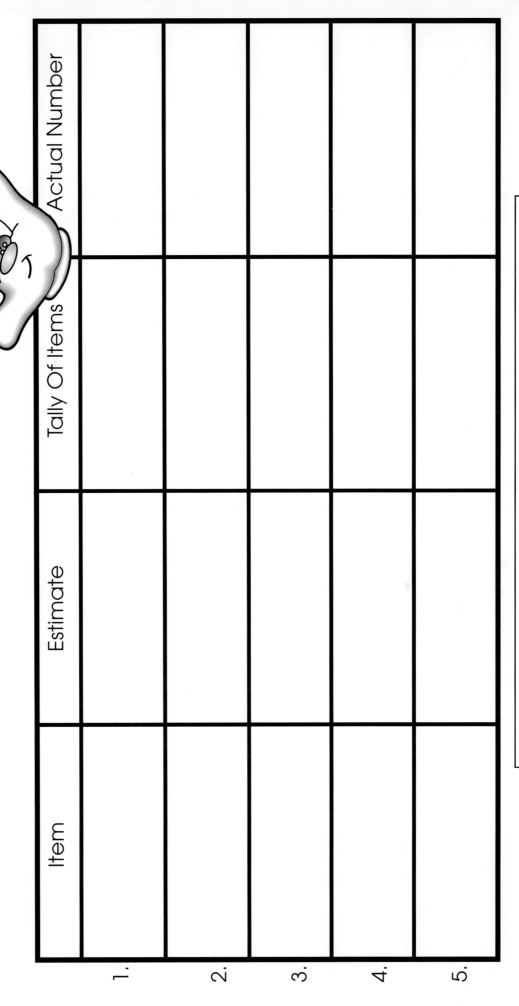

Item	Estimate	Tally Of Items	Actual Number
1.			
2.			
3.			
4.			
5.			

Bonus Box: Which item had the closest estimate? _____

©1997 The Education Center, Inc. • *Lifesaver Lessons*™ • Grade 1 • TEC503

How To Extend The Lesson:

- Take this tasty opportunity to provide students with estimation practice. Give each student a healthful snack such as a large carrot or a piece of celery. Ask each student to estimate how many bites it will take him to eat his snack. Next have the student eat his snack while making a tally mark for each bite on a piece of paper. Have the student count his tally marks and then compare his estimate to the results.

- Estimating and graphing go hand in hand! Graph predictions by organizing similar responses; then compare them to the actual results. Students will make observations like "More people thought there were fewer than 25 beans in the jar." Record comments directly on the graphs.

- For this whole-group activity, you'll need a laundry detergent scoop, a clear container to be filled, and the material (such as beans) you're pouring in the container. Pour one scoopful of the material into the container. Ask students to estimate how many scoopfuls they think it will take to fill the container to the top. Then add a few more scoopfuls and allow students to revise their predictions based on this new amount in the container. Continue in the same manner until the container is full.

- Display a chart in the classroom that features the following questions. Refer to the chart when discussing estimating activities with your students.

- What is the smallest estimate?
- What is the greatest estimate?
- What is the difference between your estimate and the actual result?
- Did you make a reasonable estimate?
- Which estimates are closest to the actual result?
- Are most of the estimates too high, too low, or just right?

Fractions By The Slice

*Whet your students' appetites for fractions with this savory lesson.
There's plenty of learning in every slice!*

Skill: Determining fractional parts—halves, thirds, and quarters

Estimated Lesson Time: 30 minutes

Teacher Preparation:
1. Duplicate page 45 and page 92 for each student.
2. Cut out three large circles and lightly color each one to resemble a pizza.

Materials:
1 copy of page 45 per student
1 copy of page 92 per student
crayons
scissors

Quick Tip:
When introducing fractions, explain to students that there are two types of fractions—candy-bar fractions (parts of a whole) and gumball fractions (parts of a set). Using both types of candy as visual aids, divide them into fractional parts and sets.

Introducing The Lesson:

Ask students, "What is round, made of dough, and yummy to eat?" Provide students with the opportunity to guess; then, if needed, provide students with the answer—pizza! Next have each student imagine that she and a friend have ordered a pizza. Ask students how the pizza could be shared fairly. Then remind students that when something is divided into fair shares, the parts are called *fractions*.

Steps:

1. Tell students that if two people want to share a pizza, it would need to be cut into halves. Cut one pizza cutout (previously made) in half. Write "$\frac{1}{2}$" on each pizza half.

2. Repeat the same process with the other two pizza cutouts—one for thirds and one for fourths.

3. Distribute copies of page 45 and page 92 to each student. Have each student color and cut out the pizzas (page 92) along the dotted lines. Then read aloud the questions on page 45 and have students answer them by comparing the pizza slices.

4. Challenge students to complete the Bonus Box activity.

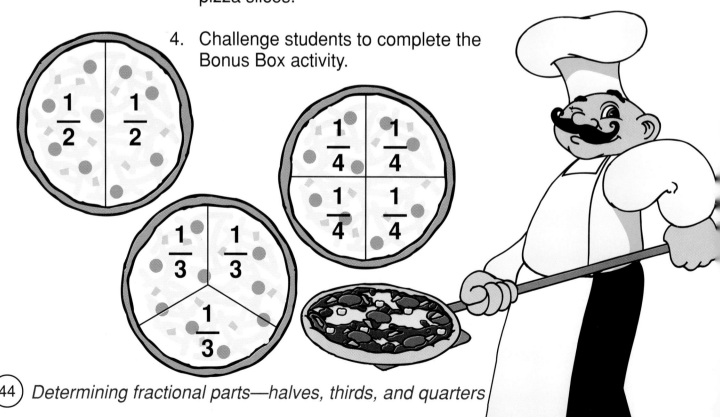

Determining fractional parts—halves, thirds, and quarters

Name_____

Fractions By The Slice

Compare the slices.
Answer the questions.

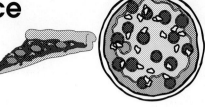

1. What is the smallest piece?   _____

2. What is the biggest piece?   _____

3. Which is more: $\frac{1}{2}$ or $\frac{1}{4}$?   _____

4. Which is less: $\frac{1}{2}$ or $\frac{1}{4}$?   _____

5. How many $\frac{1}{3}$ s would it take to make a   _____
    whole pizza?

6. How many $\frac{1}{4}$ pieces fit on a $\frac{1}{2}$ piece?   _____

7. Pam, Mark, Dan, and Pat bought a pizza.   _____
    They cut it in equal pieces. Each one
    ate a piece. How much did each of
    them eat?

8. Name the slices that are smaller than $\frac{1}{2}$.   _____

Bonus Box: On the back of this paper, draw a picture of your favorite
type of pizza.

©1997 The Education Center, Inc. • Lifesaver Lessons™ • Grade 1 • TEC503

How To Extend The Lesson:

- Extend your fractions lesson by having students make individual pizzas. Provide each child with an English muffin or a flat piece of pita bread, pizza sauce, and mozzarella cheese. Have students spoon the pizza sauce onto the bread, then sprinkle the cheese on top. Bake the miniature pizzas for 10–12 minutes at 350°; then assist students in cutting their pizzas into fractional slices.

- Supply each student with three pieces of paper. Have each child fold one piece of paper into halves, one piece of paper into thirds, and one piece of paper into fourths. For each piece of paper, instruct students to label each part with its fraction.

- For some tasty reading, share *Eating Fractions* by Bruce McMillan (Scholastic Inc., 1991), *The Doorbell Rang* by Pat Hutchins (Greenwillow, 1986), and *How Many Ways Can You Cut A Pie?* by Jane Belk Moncure (American Education Publishing, Inc.; 1993)

- This appetizing activity works well with a whole group or at a center. Provide each child with a paper plate and some construction paper. Have the student decorate her plate to look like her favorite kind of pizza. When the pizza is complete, have her decide how many people she would like to share her pizza with. Then have her cut her pizza into the correct fractional slices. To complete the activity, have the student label each slice of pizza with its fraction. If desired, display the pizzas on a bulletin board titled "Pizza Fraction Fun."

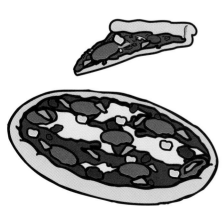

 Determining fractional parts—halves, thirds, and quarters

Delightful Days

Reinforce calendar concepts with this sunny math lesson.

Skill: Reading a calendar

Estimated Lesson Time: 30 minutes

Teacher Preparation:
1. Duplicate page 49 for each student.
2. Display a calendar for the current month.

Materials:
1 piece of drawing paper per student
crayons
1 copy of page 49 per student
1 calendar display of the current month (If a calendar is not available, one can be drawn on the chalkboard.)

Teacher Reference:
Students might refer to a calendar when determining:
• which days they will attend school
• the proximity of a birthday
• the days to attend special activities such as soccer or piano practice
• the date to write on an assignment
• the dates of holidays
• the number of days until a due date such as one for an assignment or a library book

Introducing The Lesson:

Share with the class your favorite day of the week and explain why you chose that day. Then call on each student to name his favorite day. Use tally marks to record students' responses on the chalkboard. Total the tally marks for each day to determine the class favorite.

Steps:

1. Use your calendar display to review with students how to read a calendar, the difference between the *day* and the *date,* and the order of the days of the week.

2. Ask students to name reasons they use calendars. See the list below for possible reasons.

3. Assign each child a day of the week, and provide him with a piece of drawing paper and crayons. Instruct him to write his assigned day at the top of his paper and then draw and label a picture of something he does on that day. Provide students with examples such as "go to soccer practice" or "go to the school library." Encourage each child to share his completed picture.

4. Distribute page 49 to each student.

5. Challenge each child to complete the Bonus Box activity.

JUNE

S	M	T	W	T	F	S
				1	2	3
4	5	6	7	8	9	10
11	12	13	14	15	16	17
18	19	20	21	22	23	24
25	26	27	28	29	30	

Monday, June 5
(day) (month) (date)

Reading a calendar

Delightful Days

Complete the calendar for this month.

Sunday	**Monday**	**Tuesday**	**Wednesday**	**Thursday**	**Friday**	**Saturday**

_____ _____
(month)   (year)

Use the calendar. Write the answers.

1. How many days are in this month? _____

2. Name the first day of this month. _____

3. Name the last day of this month. _____

4. What day is today's date? _____

5. How many Fridays are in this month? _____

6. Draw a 🌞 on the first Tuesday.

Bonus Box: On the back of this sheet, write what month is your favorite and explain why.

©1997 The Education Center, Inc. • *Lifesaver Lessons™* • Grade 1 • TEC503

How To Extend The Lesson:

• Teach students the abbreviation for each day of the week. Have students practice writing the abbreviations using correct capitalization and punctuation.

• Have students create alliterative booklets for the days of the week. Provide each child with a stapled booklet consisting of four pieces of paper. Have her write her name and the title of her book on the first page. On each of the other pages, have the student use the initial consonant of one of the days of the week to develop a page for that day. An example might be "On *Monday Mary made muffins* for *many monkeys.*"

• Use journal time to incorporate the days of the week into students' writing. Each day provide students with a journal-writing starter such as "Today is [day of the week], and I learned about [topic]."

• Display a calendar for the current month. Have students take turns making up riddles about the dates on the calendar, such as "I am thinking of a date that is on a Wednesday and is after the 12th."

• Delight your students with the literature selections listed below that focus on the days of the week:

—*Potatoes On Tuesday* by Dee Lillegard (GoodYearBooks, 1995)
—*Come Out And Play, Little Mouse* by Robert Kraus (Greenwillow Books, 1987)
—*Dinosaur Days* by Linda Manning (BridgeWater Books, 1993)
—*The Very Hungry Caterpillar* by Eric Carle (Philomel Books, 1994)
—*Cookie's Week* by Cindy Ward (G. P. Putnam's Sons, 1992)

Time For A Cookie Break!

Students are sure to eat up this tasty time-telling activity!

Skills: Determining the concept of one minute; telling time to the hour and half hour

Estimated Lesson Time: 40 minutes

Teacher Preparation:
1. Duplicate a class supply of cookie patterns (page 52) onto light brown construction paper.
2. Cut out the cookies and program each one with a different hour or half-hour time.
3. Duplicate page 53 for each student.
4. Draw four clocks on the chalkboard.
5. Obtain a teaching clock or use the patterns on page 93 to make one.

Materials:
light brown construction paper
scissors
black marker
teaching clock with movable hands (or the clock on page 93)
1 copy of page 53 per student
brown crayons
yellow crayons

Teacher Reference:
Activities for students to perform for one minute:
- jumping jacks
- marching in place
- writing their names
- reciting the alphabet
- drawing circles
- jumping rope
- bouncing a ball

Introducing The Lesson:

Read aloud the activities from the Teacher Reference on page 51 and have each child choose one activity. Then time students as they each determine the number of repetitions of their chosen activity that they can perform in one minute. Invite students to share their results with the class. If desired, time students in one-minute intervals as they count repetitions for other activities listed in the Teacher Reference.

Steps:

1. Review the concepts of the *minute hand* and the *hour hand* with students using the teaching clock.

2. Distribute a labeled cookie cutout to each student.

3. Ask four children to draw hands on the clock faces to show the times written on their cookies. After checking the hands, have each of the four students ask a classmate to write on the chalkboard the time shown. Erase the clock hands and their corresponding times; then have four additional students draw hands on a clock. Continue in this same manner until each student has had a turn to draw hands on a clock.

4. Distribute a copy of page 53 to each student.

5. Challenge students to complete the Bonus Box activity.

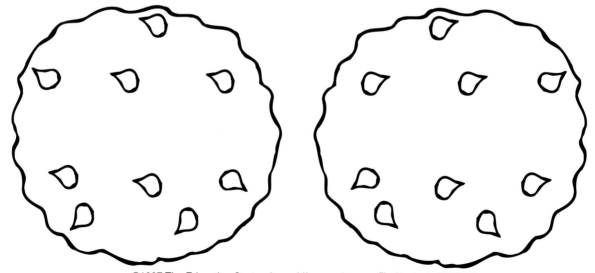

©1997 The Education Center, Inc. • *Lifesaver Lessons*™ • Grade 1 • TEC503

Determining the concept of one minute; telling time to the hour and half hour

Name _____

Time For A Cookie Break!

Write the time under each cookie.

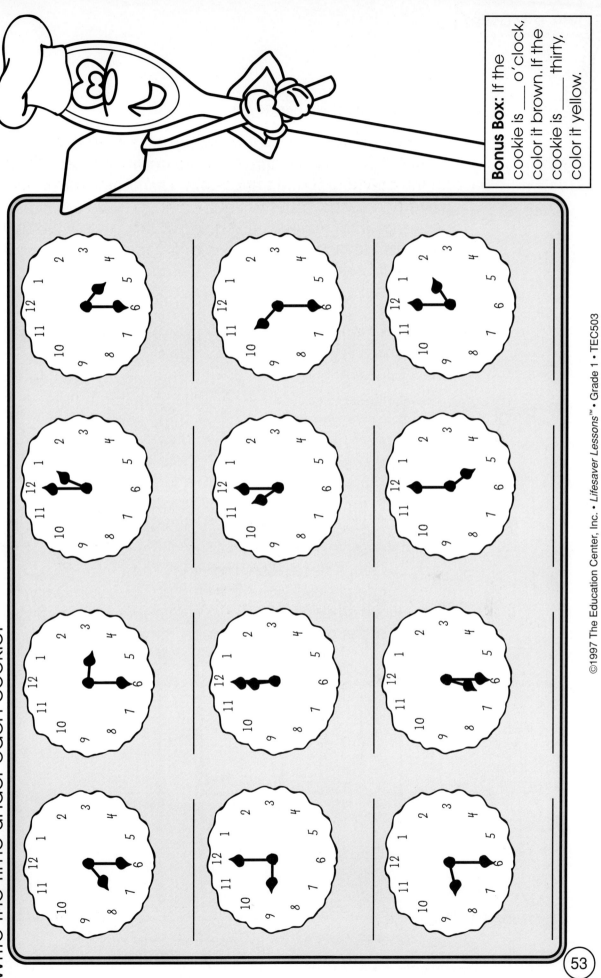

©1997 The Education Center, Inc. • Lifesaver Lessons™ • Grade 1 • TEC503

Bonus Box: If the cookie is _____ o'clock, color it brown. If the cookie is _____ thirty, color it yellow.

53

How To Extend The Lesson:

• Review morning and evening activities with this activity. Label a class supply of index cards with different times of the day (including hours, half hours, A.M., and P.M.). Distribute one of the cards and a piece of drawing paper to each student. Have each student draw a picture of what he is usually doing at this time of the day. Then instruct him to label his picture with a sentence such as "At 8:00 P.M. I am getting ready to go to bed." Compile the pages into a class book titled "What's The Time?"

• Challenge students to brainstorm sayings with the word *time* in them. Record their responses on the chalkboard. Possible additions:

In the nick of time	The time of your life
Time flies	Once upon a time
Time marches on	Time is money
Time on my hands	Time's up
Passing the time of day	Killing time
For the time being	On time
Wasting time	The big time

• Duplicate copies of the Daily Time Check slip below. Attach a slip to each student's desk every morning. Then throughout the day declare, "Time check!" Write the time on your own Daily Time Check sheet while students check the classroom clock and log the time. At the end of the day, check students' times during a group review.

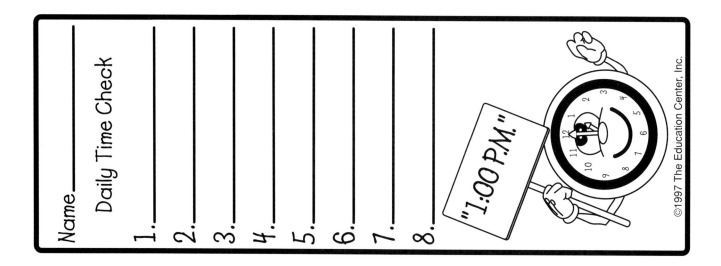

Determining the concept of one minute; telling time to the hour and half hour

Ahoy, Mateys!

Your young buccaneers will discover a wealth of money skills with this swashbuckling lesson.

Skill: Counting coin combinations to 50¢ (dime, nickel, penny)

Estimated Lesson Time: 40 minutes

Teacher Preparation:
1. Place a real nickel, dime, and penny in a small paper bag.
2. Secure a supply of real, plastic, or paper coins for each student. (See page 95 for coin reproducibles.)
3. Duplicate the cube pattern on page 94 for each student pair.
4. Duplicate page 57 for each student pair.

Materials:
1 copy of page 57 per student pair
1 copy of page 94 per student pair
small paper bag
1 real penny, 1 real nickel, and 1 real dime
supply of real, plastic, or paper coins
scissors

Teacher Reference:
Coin facts to share:
- A nickel is bigger than a penny or a dime.
- The dime and penny are almost the same size.
- The penny and the nickel have smooth edges.
- Dimes, quarters, half-dollars, and dollars have ridges called *milling* or *reeding* to help blind people recognize certain denominations.
- Abraham Lincoln is on the heads side of the penny.
- Thomas Jefferson is on the heads side of the nickel.
- Franklin D. Roosevelt is on the heads side of the dime.

Introducing The Lesson:

Tell students that while digging in your backyard you discovered a bag of coins. (Display the paper bag for students to see.) Ask a student volunteer to reach into the bag, feel the coins, and guess the name of each coin. Have the child take the coins out of the bag, one at a time, to verify his guesses.

Steps:

1. Share with students the coin facts from the Teacher Reference on page 55. Then ask a different student volunteer to repeat the activity in the introduction of this lesson.

2. Distribute a supply of real, plastic, or paper coins to each student. Have students study the heads and tails of each coin. Then review with students the values of pennies, nickels, and dimes.

3. Pair students; then give each student pair a copy of page 57 and a cube pattern from page 94. Assist students in creating their cubes.

4. To play the game, one student in each pair rolls the cube and records the value of the coin shown in the column labeled "Roll 1." The other partner then follows in the same manner. The players continue, alternating rolls, until they have each recorded the values shown from five rolls of the cube. Each player then totals his rolls and writes the total amount of money in the "Total" column. The player with the highest total wins that round.

5. Have your buccaneers repeat the activity in the same manner for four additional rounds.

Ahoy, Mateys!

Names	Roll 1	Roll 2	Roll 3	Roll 4	Roll 5	Total
Katelyn	10¢	5¢	5¢	10¢	1¢	31¢
Matt	5¢	1¢	10¢	10¢	1¢	27¢
Katelyn	10¢	5¢	1¢	5¢	1¢	22¢

Ahoy, Mateys!

Names	Roll 1	Roll 2	Roll 3	Roll 4	Roll 5	Total
1.						
2.						
3.						
4.						
5.						

©1997 The Education Center, Inc. • *Lifesaver Lessons*™ • Grade 1 • TEC503

How To Extend The Lesson:

- Share the following money expressions with your students:
  "Penny pincher"—a person who doesn't like to spend his money
  "Red cent"—your last penny
  "You look like a million bucks!"—You look terrific!
  "Two cents worth"—an opinion a person feels he must give
  "A penny for your thoughts"—what you say when you want to know what someone is thinking
  "Your bottom dollar"—the lowest price
  "Dime a dozen"—a cheap deal
  "A penny saved is a penny earned."—Saving money is just like earning it.
  "Money doesn't grow on trees."—You must work hard for money.
  "Save for a rainy day."—Save your money for a time when you really need it.

- Divide students into small groups for this cooperative-group activity. For each student group, label an index card—each with a different amount of money (less than 50¢). Provide each group with an index card and a supply of dimes, nickels, and pennies. Have each group of students work together to show as many different coin combinations as possible for the amount on each index card.

- Read *Why Money Was Invented* by Neale S. Godfrey (Silver Burdett Press, 1996) to your students. This delightful picture book explains the invention of money, beginning with the concept of trading to obtain goods.

- Duplicate a class supply of the award shown below. Then glue each child's photograph on a copy of the award.

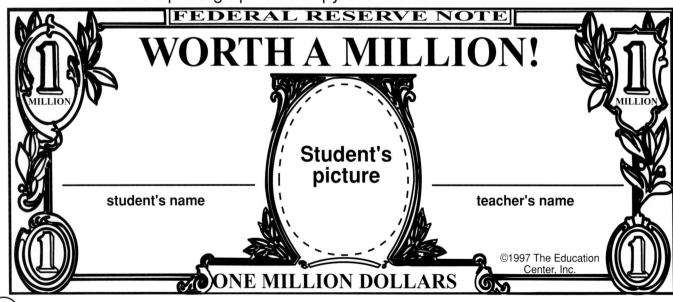

FEDERAL RESERVE NOTE

WORTH A MILLION!

1 MILLION   1 MILLION

Student's picture

_____
student's name

_____
teacher's name

©1997 The Education Center, Inc.

ONE MILLION DOLLARS

Counting coin combinations to 50¢ (dime, nickel, penny)

Bakery Buys

Treat your students to a delectable money lesson that's filled with cakes, pies, doughnuts, and more!

Skill: Making coin combinations to 99¢ (dime, nickel, penny)

Estimated Lesson Time: 45 minutes

Teacher Preparation:
1. Provide a supply of real, plastic, or paper coins to each pair of students. (See page 95 for coin reproducibles.)
2. Duplicate page 61 for each student.

Materials:
supply of real, paper, or plastic coins
1 copy of page 61 per student
1 sheet of drawing paper per pair of students

Introducing The Lesson:

Ask students to name foods found in a bakery. Record their responses on the chalkboard. Then tell students that they are going to purchase some pastries today in their math lesson.

Steps:

1. Pair students; then distribute a piece of drawing paper to each student pair. Assign a different bakery item from the list for each pair to draw.

2. Collect the completed pictures and label each bakery item with a price.

3. Redistribute a bakery-item picture and a supply of dimes, nickels, and pennies to each student pair.

4. Instruct each pair of students to cooperatively use the coins to show the stated amount. Rotate around the classroom to check students' work.

5. After a designated amount of time, have each student pair exchange pictures with another pair and repeat the activity. Continue in this manner until each student pair has worked with each picture.

6. Distribute a copy of page 61 to each student.

7. Challenge students to complete the Bonus Box activity.

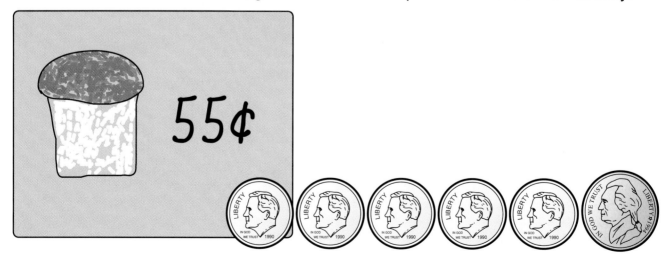

Making coin combinations to 99¢ (dime, nickel, penny)

Name _____

Bakery Buys

Bakery

doughnut
28¢

turnover
62¢

pie
45¢

roll
76¢

cupcake
81¢

Write how much is shown.
Write what you can buy on the line.

1.

_____¢ I can buy the _____.

2.

_____¢ I can buy the _____.

3.

_____¢ I can buy the _____.

4.

_____¢ I can buy the _____.

5.

_____¢ I can buy the _____.

Bonus Box: Write the bakery items in order from most expensive to least expensive.

©1997 The Education Center, Inc. • Lifesaver Lessons™ • Grade 1 • TEC503

How To Extend The Lesson:

• Create a classroom store! Stock an area of the classroom with stickers, pencils, and other small, inexpensive items; then label each item with a price. Award monetary points to each table or group of students for working well together. (For example, if one table has earned 45¢ at the end of the week, each person at that table receives 45¢ in plastic or cut-out coins.) Students can either spend their money earned that week at the store or save their money to purchase more expensive items the next week.

• Share some of these valuable stories with your youngsters:
  —*A Chair For My Mother* by Vera B. Williams (Greenwillow Books, 1982)
  —*General Store* by Rachel Field (Little, Brown & Company; 1988)
  —*If You Made A Million* by David M. Schwartz (Morrow Junior Books, 1994)
  —*Our Garage Sale* by Anne Rockwell (Greenwillow Books, 1984)
  —*Alexander, Who Used To Be Rich Last Sunday* by Judith Viorst (Aladdin Paperbacks, 1987)

• Instruct each student to cut a picture from a magazine of an item such as clothing, a toy, or food. Collect the pictures and mount them on a bulletin board. Assign prices to the items; then write each item's price on a price tag. Mount each price tag below its item. Then discuss the prices of the objects shown on the bulletin board, using questions such as "Which object costs the most?", "Which item costs the least?", and "Which object costs less than three dimes?"

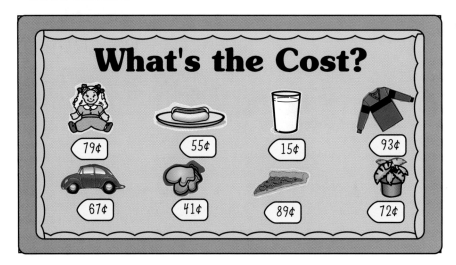

No Rulers Allowed!

Rule out the rulers with this activity featuring nonstandard measurement.

Skill: Measuring in nonstandard units

Estimated Lesson Time: 30 minutes

Teacher Preparation:

Duplicate page 65 for each student.

Materials:

large paper clips
small paper clips
1 container of large and small paper clips mixed together
1 unsharpened pencil
1 copy of page 65 per student

Teacher Reference:

Additional nonstandard units that students
   can use as measurement tools:
Unifix® cubes
footprints
handprints
unsharpened pencils
crayons of the same length
paintbrushes
pens
string

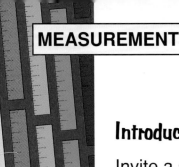

Introducing The Lesson:

Invite a student volunteer to help you measure the length of an unsharpened pencil. Provide the student with a box of large and small paper clips and ask him to use the paper clips to measure the length of the pencil. Record the student's finding (such as three large paper clips and one small paper clip) on the chalkboard; then repeat the procedure with other students.

Steps:

1. After recording at least five measurements on the chalkboard, point out to students that the measurements are different. Lead them to understand the importance of measuring with units of the same size.

2. Distribute a copy of page 65 and some large and small paper clips to each student.

3. Instruct students to write "large paper clips" on the first line labeled "Unit" and "small paper clips" on the other line labeled "Unit."

4. Ask each student to choose four items from his desk or around the room to measure. Have him draw and label each of the items in a different box on the left-hand side of his paper.

5. Instruct each student to measure each of his four items, first using the large paper clips and then the small paper clips. Have him record each measurement in its appropriate place on the reproducible.

6. Challenge students to complete the Bonus Box activity.

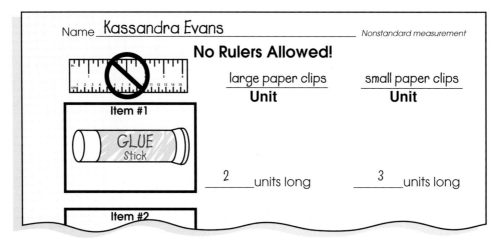

No Rulers Allowed!

_____   _____
Unit   Unit

Item #1

_____units long   _____units long

Item #2

_____units long   _____units long

Item #3

_____units long   _____units long

Item #4

_____units long   _____units long

Bonus Box: For each item, find the difference between the number of large and small paper clips used. Record your answers on the back of this paper.

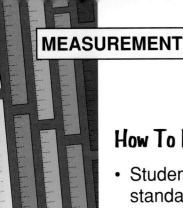

How To Extend The Lesson:

- Students only need a supply of Unifix® cubes and a partner for this non-standard measurement center. As each student visits the center, he estimates how many Unifix® cubes tall he is; then he lays down on the ground as his partner checks the estimate by interlocking the cubes until they are equal to his height. To count the cubes used, have students break off ten cubes at a time and count by tens.

- Share with your students *The Fattest, Tallest, Biggest Snowman Ever* by Bettina Ling (Scholastic Inc., 1997). In this Hello Math Reader™, two children use nonstandard measurements to try to determine who built the biggest snowman.

- Have students use paper clips to take different measurements on their bodies such as:
    How many paper clips long is your arm?
    How many paper clips wide is your hand?
    How many paper clips long is your foot?
    How many paper clips fit around your wrist?
    How many paper clips long is your thumb?

- Use your footprint or the principal's footprint to create measurement excitement! Trace the outline of your foot or your principal's foot onto tagboard and cut out the resulting shape. Have each child use the template to create a construction-paper replica. Next have each student draw a picture of an item in the classroom, measure the item with the footprint, and then record the measurement beside the illustration. Mount these drawings on a bulletin board labeled "Step By Step With [your name or your principal's name]."

Down On The Farm

Take your youngsters on an imaginary journey to a hay-strewn, animal-filled barnyard for practice with measurement.

Skill: Measuring inches with a ruler

Estimated Lesson Time: 25 minutes

Teacher Preparation:

1. Draw a map similar to the one shown below on a large sheet of bulletin-board paper. Be sure that the distance between every pair of points can be measured in exact inches and that no distance is longer than 12 inches.
2. Duplicate page 69 for each student.
3. Obtain a class supply of rulers. Or duplicate the ruler on page 68 for each student.

Materials:

1 piece of paper: any size
several paper clips and crayons
1 large piece of bulletin-board paper
1 ruler per student (or 1 copy of the ruler on page 68 per student)
1 copy of page 69 per student
marker
one 12-inch ruler

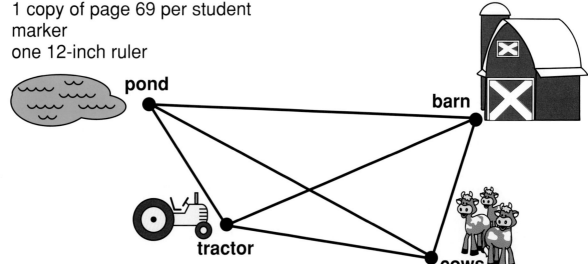

Introducing The Lesson:

Tell students that you need to know the length of a piece of paper. As students watch, measure the paper using a variety of mixed units, such as paper clips and crayons. Once you determine the approximate length of the paper, share your findings with the class (for example, "The paper is two paper clips and three crayons long."). Then ask students if they know an easier way to measure the paper. Lead students to the solution of using a ruler to measure the paper in inches.

Steps:

1. Display the large map for students to see. Announce two points on the map, such as the pond and the barn. Call on a student volunteer to come to the map and use a 12-inch ruler to measure the distance between the two points. Write the number of inches on the line that stretches between the two points. Repeat the activity until all distances have been measured.

2. Distribute a 12-inch or 6-inch ruler and a copy of page 69 to each student.

3. Challenge students to complete the Bonus Box activity.

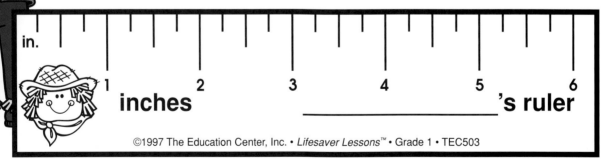

in. | 1 **inches** 2 | 3 | 4 | 5 | 6 _____'s ruler

©1997 The Education Center, Inc. • *Lifesaver Lessons™* • Grade 1 • TEC503

in. | 1 **inches** 2 | 3 | 4 | 5 **'s ruler** 6

©1997 The Education Center, Inc. • *Lifesaver Lessons™* • Grade 1 • TEC503

Down On The Farm

Measure each line.
Write the length in the box.

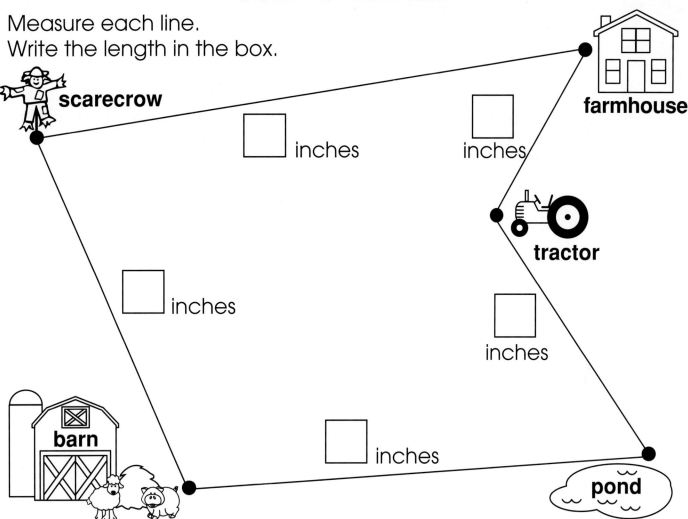

Write the distance between the items.

1. [tractor] and [pond] _____ inches

2. [scarecrow] and [barn] _____ inches

3. [scarecrow] and [farmhouse] _____ inches

4. [barn] and [pond] _____ inches

5. [tractor] and [farmhouse] _____ inches

Bonus Box: What is the distance in inches around the whole farm? _____

©1997 The Education Center, Inc. • *Lifesaver Lessons*™ • Grade 1 • TEC503

How To Extend The Lesson:

- Have students create a class measurement book featuring inches. For each child use a ruler to draw one line—an exact number of inches long—on a piece of drawing paper. Be sure to make the lines in a variety of lengths on the papers. Add a dot at each end of each line. Then instruct each student to transform his line into an item that is its exact length. Then have each child write "My [item name] is [number] inches long" on his paper. Compile students' pages into a class book titled "Wacky Measurement." Use a length of yarn to attach a laminated paper ruler to the book's binding. Students will enjoy using the ruler to measure their classmates' items in the book.

- Create a colorful measurement center that is sure to capture students' interest. To make the center, cut various lengths of different-colored yarn; then design and duplicate a class supply of a fill-in-the-blank reproducible that requires students to record the length of each color of yarn. ("The [color] yarn is [number] inches long.") Provide students with rulers or copies of a ruler (page 68) to use at this center.

- Design a reproducible with lines of various lengths in inches. Reproduce a class supply and distribute one sheet to each child. Ask each child to first write an estimate of each line's measurement with a crayon. Then have the child measure each line with a ruler and write the answer in pencil beside the estimate.

- Duplicate copies of the award shown below for your students.

_____
student

really measures up!

_____
teacher

©1997 The Education Center, Inc. • *Lifesaver Lessons™* • Grade 1 • TEC503

Measuring Up

Just for good measure, size up your students' measurement skills with this lesson on centimeters.

Skills: Estimating centimeters; measuring centimeters with a ruler

Estimated Lesson Time: 30 minutes

Teacher Preparation:

1. Duplicate page 73 for each student.
2. Obtain a class supply of centimeter rulers. Or duplicate the ruler on page 72 for each student.
3. Gather several small items to measure, such as a paper clip, a crayon, a piece of tape, a glue bottle, and a piece of chalk.

Materials:

1 copy of page 73 per student
1 centimeter ruler per student
several small items to measure

Quick Tip: To help students who are having difficulty reading a ruler, visually divide the units on the rulers by coloring each unit a different color.

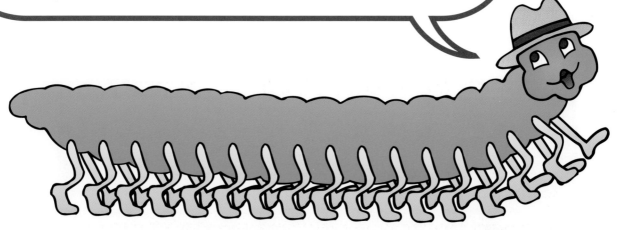

Introducing The Lesson:

Make a list on the chalkboard of several small classroom objects, such as a paper clip, a crayon, a piece of tape, a glue bottle, and a piece of chalk. Have students estimate the length in centimeters of each of the objects. Record the estimates of several volunteers.

Steps:

1. Enlist student volunteers to help you measure the objects to the nearest centimeter. Compare the measurements with the estimations.

2. Have students brainstorm a list of activities that require exact measurements, such as making a dress or building a house. Then have students brainstorm a second list of activities that require only estimated measurements.

3. Distribute a ruler and a copy of page 73 to each student.

4. Challenge students to complete the Bonus Box activity.

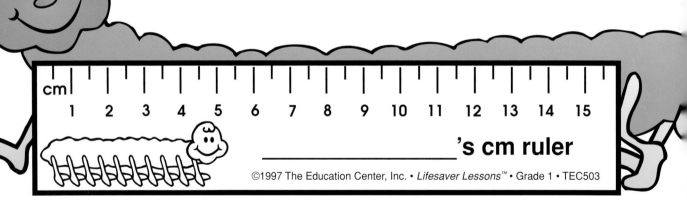

_____'s cm ruler

©1997 The Education Center, Inc. • *Lifesaver Lessons*™ • Grade 1 • TEC503

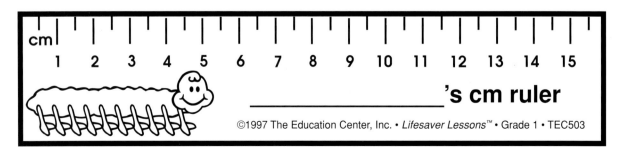

_____'s cm ruler

©1997 The Education Center, Inc. • *Lifesaver Lessons*™ • Grade 1 • TEC503

Measuring Up

Measure.
Write how long.

1. 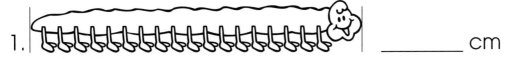 _____ cm

2.  _____ cm

3.  _____ cm

4.  _____ cm

Guess the length of each object.
Measure to find the length.

Things to measure in centimeters	My guess	My measurement	Color the 🐛 for each correct guess.
a crayon			
a paper clip			
my pencil			
my hand 🖐️			
a glue bottle GLUE			
my thumb			

Bonus Box: Find as many things as possible in the classroom that are 10 cm long. Write them on the back of this paper.

73

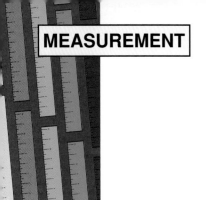

How To Extend The Lesson:

• Use string or yarn to measure a common characteristic of each child, such as his index finger. Put a piece of masking tape labeled with the student's name on each string. Compare lengths of strings. Remeasure with a centimeter ruler.

• Provide each student with a piece of shoestring licorice and a plastic knife. Instruct each student to measure how long her piece is. Then ask her to cut off a specific centimeter length of the licorice, such as a piece that is seven centimeters long. What a tasty way to practice measurement!

• Have each student make a list of objects that measure about one centimeter. Suggest that students measure the space between the lines on their notebook paper, the width of a pencil, the width of a staple, and the width of a straw.

• Choose several small objects and write the length of each object in centimeters on a separate index card. Place the objects and the cards on a table. (Turn the cards facedown.) Ask student volunteers—one at a time—to turn over a card and match the length to the appropriate object. Then have the child verify his measurement with a centimeter ruler.

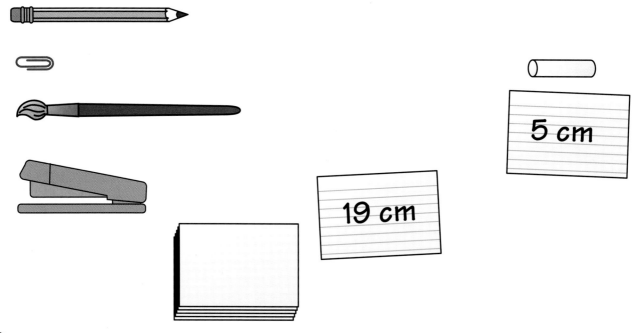

Estimating centimeters; measuring centimeters with a ruler

Pocketful Of Patterns

What can you pull out of your pocket?
Plenty of practice with patterns, that's what!

Skill: Recognizing patterns

Estimated Lesson Time: 30 minutes

Teacher Preparation:

1. Collect three different types of objects—such as paper clips, pennies, and craft sticks—to use in creating patterns. Place one of each of the three objects in your pockets. If you are not wearing clothing with pockets, place the three objects in an envelope and draw a pocket on it.
2. Set up an overhead projector.
3. Duplicate page 77 for each student.

Materials:

several small objects to use in creating patterns
overhead projector
1 copy of page 77 per student
one 9" x 12" piece of colored construction paper
  per student
scissors
glue
crayons

Teacher Reference:

Four basic patterns are:

AB   ABC   ABB   AAB

Introducing The Lesson:

Tell students that they are going to use whatever objects are in your pockets to complete today's math lesson. Ask students to guess your pockets' contents. After several guesses, remove the three objects from your pockets.

Steps:

1. Using the overhead projector and the three different types of objects, make an AB, ABB, AAB, or ABC pattern on the screen. Ask a student volunteer to identify the pattern and then continue it on the screen.

2. Next have the student who correctly names and continues the pattern to use the objects to create another pattern. Then have the student call on a classmate to identify the pattern and continue it. That classmate then gets a turn to create the next pattern. Continue in this manner until students have a good understanding of the different patterns.

3. Distribute a copy of page 77 and a piece of construction paper to each student. Instruct students to cut out the pockets and glue them to the paper in three different patterns. If desired, have students label each of their patterns and color them accordingly.

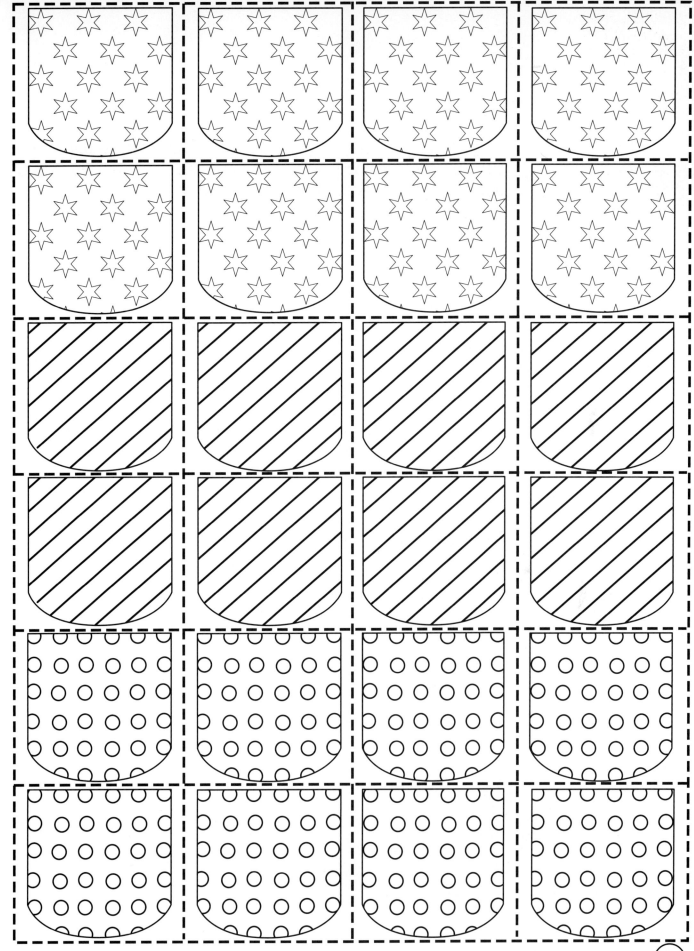

©1997 The Education Center, Inc. • *Lifesaver Lessons*™ • Grade 1 • TEC503

How To Extend The Lesson:

- Have students use letters of the alphabet to create patterns. Encourage patterns that review concepts such as vowels, consonants, uppercase letters, or lowercase letters.

- Ask students to brainstorm ideas for a class pattern. (Some examples are boy-girl, hair color or length, color of clothing, and eye color.) Line up students to create the pattern ideas. Reverse the activity by lining up students in a certain order and then having them identify the pattern shown.

- Reinforce patterning concepts in a tasty way! Provide students with grapes, strawberries, and chunks of pineapples and cheese. Have students make pattern snacks by putting fruit and cheese chunks onto shish kebab skewers. Encourage youngsters to name their classmates' patterns and predict what comes next.

- Take students on a pattern walk around the school. Upon returning to the classroom, have students name places where they saw patterns.

Patterns we saw at school:
- cars in the parking lot
- U.S. flag
- bricks in the wall
- wallpaper in the office
- floor tiles
- the quilt hanging near the cafeteria

Monkeying Around

Students are sure to have a ball with this math lesson featuring logic problems.

Skill: Solving logic problems

Estimated Lesson Time: 40 minutes

Teacher Preparation:
Duplicate page 81 for each student.

Materials:
1 copy of page 81 per student
stapler
tape dispenser
glue bottle
scissors for each student
red, yellow, and blue crayons for each student
miscellaneous small classroom items

Teacher Reference:
The following list shows all possible combinations for arranging three objects:
first item, second item, third item
first item, third item, second item
second item, first item, third item
second item, third item, first item
third item, first item, second item
third item, second item, first item

Introducing The Lesson:

Place the stapler, the tape dispenser, and the glue bottle in a row on a table so that all students can see the items. Announce and record the order of the items on the chalkboard. Then ask a student to change the position of the items in the line. Announce and record the new positions of the items. Have different students continue in this same manner until all the possible combinations of positions have been shown.

Steps:

1. Remind students that it is important to change the order of the items in a pattern so that they can determine all the possible combinations. For example a student should find the two position combinations with the stapler in the first spot, then find the two combinations with the tape dispenser first, and then find the two combinations with the glue bottle first.

2. Pair students; then ask each pair to find three small items in the classroom and bring these items to their work area. Have each pair of students work together to find and record the six possible position combinations of the three items. Invite one or two pairs of students to share their findings.

3. Have students return the items they borrowed.

4. Distribute a copy of page 81 to each student.

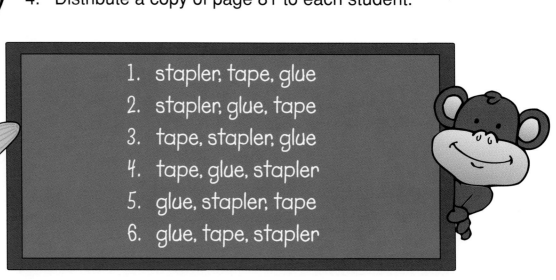

1. stapler, tape, glue
2. stapler, glue, tape
3. tape, stapler, glue
4. tape, glue, stapler
5. glue, stapler, tape
6. glue, tape, stapler

Monkeying Around

Cut out the monkeys below.
Color each ball to match its color word.

Put the monkeys in a row.
Color the balls in one row to show the order of
  the monkeys.
Do this five more times.
Make sure no rows are the same.

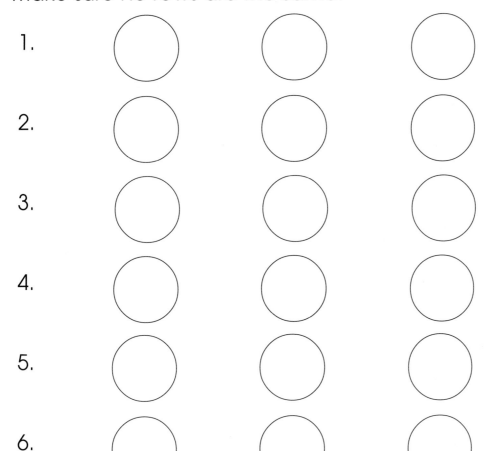

1.
2.
3.
4.
5.
6.

©1997 The Education Center, Inc. • *Lifesaver Lessons*™ • Grade 1 • TEC503

red   yellow   blue

How To Extend The Lesson:

• Supply each child with three M&M's® in different colors. Challenge each child to find and record the six different color combinations of his candies. After checking each child's answers, provide students with additional candies to eat.

• Challenge students to determine different addition combinations that add up to ten. Have each child fold a piece of drawing paper into fourths and label ten index-card halves with numerals from zero to nine. Instruct students to find four numbers that add up to ten, place each of these numerals on a different fourth of the paper, and then record the addition sentence on their papers. Have students continue to arrange the numbers on the paper and record the addition sentences for a predetermined amount of time. To conclude invite student volunteers to share their answers as you record their responses on the chalkboard.

• Draw four houses on the chalkboard like the ones shown below. Tell the students that they are to listen to the following clues to help them answer the following questions:
   Which house is Martha Monkey's?
      Martha's house has a chimney.
      Martha's house has three windows.
      Martha's house does not have a bush in front of it.
   Which house is Morton Monkey's?
      Morton's house has a bush in front of it.
      Morton's house has two windows.
      Morton's house does not have a chimney.

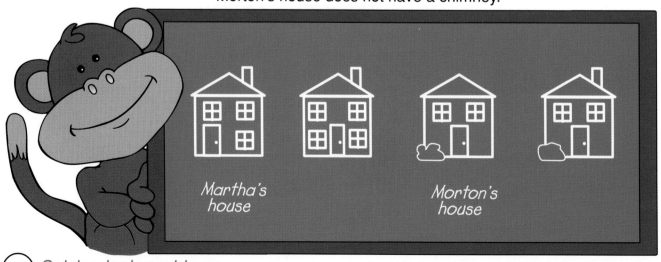

Martha's
house

Morton's
house

Order Up!

*Order some problem-solving practice for your students
with this tasty graphing activity!*

Skills: Making and using a bar graph; counting with tally marks

Estimated Lesson Time: 30 minutes

Teacher Preparation:

1. Write "Welcome To [<u>your name</u>]'s Ice-Cream Shop" on the chalk-board.
2. On the chalkboard make a blank bar graph similar to the one on page 85. Replace the four food pictures and words with the four ice-cream treats listed on the menu shown on page 84.
3. On a piece of poster board, draw a menu like the one on page 84.
4. Duplicate page 85 for each student.

Materials:

1 menu drawn on poster board
1 copy of page 85 per student
1 small notepad and a pen or pencil
crayons

Teacher Reference:

General Graphing Questions

Which row has the least?
Which row has the most?
Are there more _____ or _____?
Are there less _____ or _____?
How many _____ are there?
How many more _____ are there than _____?
How many less _____ are there than _____?
Are there any rows with the same number of squares colored?
What does this graph represent?

Introducing The Lesson:

Welcome students to your ice-cream shop. Display the poster-board menu for everyone to see; then read it aloud. Ask students to decide which type of ice-cream treat they would like to order. Pretending to be a waitress, use tally marks to record children's responses on the small notepad.

Steps:

1. Tell students that you used tally marks to record their responses on your notepad; then transfer the information to the chalkboard.

2. Demonstrate to students how to use this information to complete the bar graph. For each ice-cream treat, have students count the tally marks, and then record the answer by coloring that number of blocks on the graph.

3. Have students use the completed bar graph to answer questions, such as "What ice-cream treat was ordered the most?" or "How many people ordered that treat?" See page 83 for a list of general graphing questions.

4. Divide students into groups of no more than ten students.

5. Distribute a copy of page 85 to each student.

6. Challenge students to complete the Bonus Box activity.

7. Have a student volunteer from each group share the food his group likes best.

Menu

Ice-Cream Cones

Jumbo Banana Splits

Milkshakes

Sundaes

Making and using a bar graph

Order Up!

Work with a group of classmates.
Ask which food each classmate in the group likes best.
Use tally marks to count.

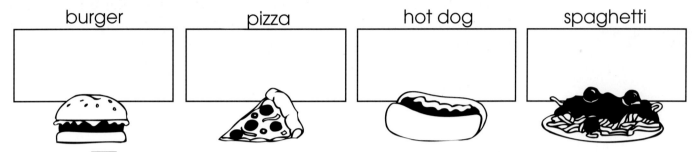

burger   pizza   hot dog   spaghetti

Color a ☐ for each tally mark.

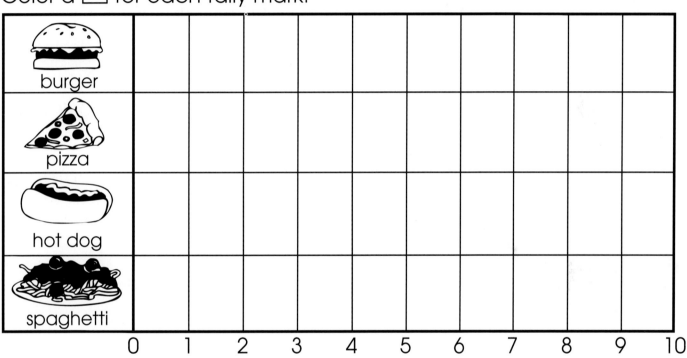

0 1 2 3 4 5 6 7 8 9 10

Write.

1. Which food did your group like best? _____

2. How many in your group chose this food? _____

3. Which food did your group like least? _____

4. How many in your group chose this food? _____

Bonus Box: Ask ten classmates what their favorite colors are. Use tally marks to record their answers.

85

©1997 The Education Center, Inc. • *Lifesaver Lessons*™ • Grade 1 • TEC503

How To Extend The Lesson:

- Design a reproducible, similar to the one on page 85, for students to use to determine the class's favorite outdoor activity, learning center, or school subject area.

- Have each student use graphing paper to create individual graphs. Instruct students to graph items, such as how many sunny, rainy, or cloudy days in a month; how many pieces of paper they use each day for a week; and which color of crayon they use the most in one day.

- Start each day with a class graph. Design a large bar graph and laminate for durability. Each morning write a question on the chalkboard (see below for examples), and use a wipe-off marker to program the graph with the items being graphed. As each student enters the classroom, have him answer the question by using the marker to write his initials in a square on the graph. After reviewing the results of the graph, simply use a damp cloth to clean the graph.

What is your favorite color?

How did you get to school today?

How many siblings do you have?

How many letters are in your first name?

How many pockets do you have?

Do your shoes have Velcro®, shoelaces, both, or neither?

What color is your hair?

How many buttons do you have?

What is your favorite fruit?

How many vowels are in your first name?

Fun At The Park!

Take your students on an imaginary trip to the park for a fun-filled lesson on story problems.

Skill: Solving and writing story problems

Estimated Lesson Time: 35 minutes

Teacher Preparation:

1. Duplicate page 89 for each student.
2. Create a transparency of page 89.
3. Cut apart the transparent bear manipulatives and color them with a permanent marker.
4. Set up an overhead projector.

Materials:

1 copy of page 89 per student
1 transparency of page 89
overhead projector
chart paper
scissors
crayons

Teacher Reference:

Incorporate word problems when students are:
• reviewing problem-solving strategies.
• practicing operational skills.
• working in partner or cooperative groups.

PLEASE DON'T
FEED
THE ANIMALS

Introducing The Lesson:

Display the overhead transparency of the park and the bear cutouts. Ask students to brainstorm activities the bears might do at the park. Record students' responses on chart paper.

Steps:

1. Choose an activity on the chart to use in creating a word problem about the bears. Have a student volunteer use the bear manipulatives to act out the problem on the overhead projector. After she has solved the problem, have her state the corresponding number sentence.

2. Distribute a copy of page 89 to each student. Instruct students to cut out and color the bear manipulatives.

3. Choose another activity from the chart to use in creating a word problem about the bears. Use the overhead manipulatives to act out the word problem as students follow along with their own manipulatives. Continue to choose activities from the chart to create additional word problems for students to model with their manipulatives.

4. Once students are able to solve and restate problems, provide ten minutes for students to work in pairs to create and solve oral story problems.

5. Instruct each student to write her favorite story problem on the reproducible. Have her glue on the bears to match the story problem and then color the picture.

Four bears were swimming in the lake. One bear was cold so he got out. How many bears were left in the lake?

The bears might:
- swing
- swim
- ride bikes
- go down the slide
- climb a tree
- play in the sandbox
- play tag
- fly a kite

88 *Solving and writing story problems*

Fun At The Park!

©1997 The Education Center, Inc. • *Lifesaver Lessons*™ • Grade 1 • TEC503

How To Extend The Lesson:

• Have students create paper-plate bear faces to use in acting out the story problems created on page 89.

• Assemble students' completed story problems into a class book to share at storytime. Students will enjoy the chance to solve their classmates' problems.

• Provide students with Gummy® Bears or Teddy Grahams® to use in modeling and solving story problems.

• Integrate math and literature by sharing one of the following bear stories:
— *Alaska's Three Bears* by Shelly R. Gill (Paws Four Publishing, 1992)
— *Berlioz The Bear* by Jan Brett (Putnam Publishing Group, 1991)
— *Ira Sleeps Over* by Bernard Waber (Houghton Mifflin Company, 1973)
— *Where's My Teddy?* by Jez Alborough (Candlewick Press, 1993)

• Provide students with problem-solving practice using this word-problem activity. Label three lunch-size paper bags as follows: "Names," "Numbers," and "Objects." Place paper strips labeled with students' names in the "Names" bag and paper strips labeled with numerals in the "Numbers" bag. Place a variety of small objects (such as a box of crayons, a pencil, an eraser, and a few small toys) in the "Objects" bag. Have a student draw two names, two numerals, and one object from the bags. List the information drawn on the board; then choose either an addition or a subtraction function. Using this information, help students create and solve a variety of word problems.

Lisa saw 5 blue cars.

David saw 3 blue cars.

How many cars did they see in all?

Names

Lisa

David

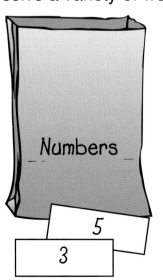

Numbers

5

3

Objects

1	2	3	4	5	6	7	8	9	10
11	12	13	14	15	16	17	18	19	20
21	22	23	24	25	26	27	28	29	30
31	32	33	34	35	36	37	38	39	40
41	42	43	44	45	46	47	48	49	50
51	52	53	54	55	56	57	58	59	60
61	62	63	64	65	66	67	68	69	70
71	72	73	74	75	76	77	78	79	80
81	82	83	84	85	86	87	88	89	90
91	92	93	94	95	96	97	98	99	100

©1997 The Education Center, Inc. • *Lifesaver Lessons*™ • Grade 1 • TEC503

Note To Teacher: Use with "Hopping Down The Number Trail" on page 31.

Color.
Cut out the pizzas.
Cut apart the slices.

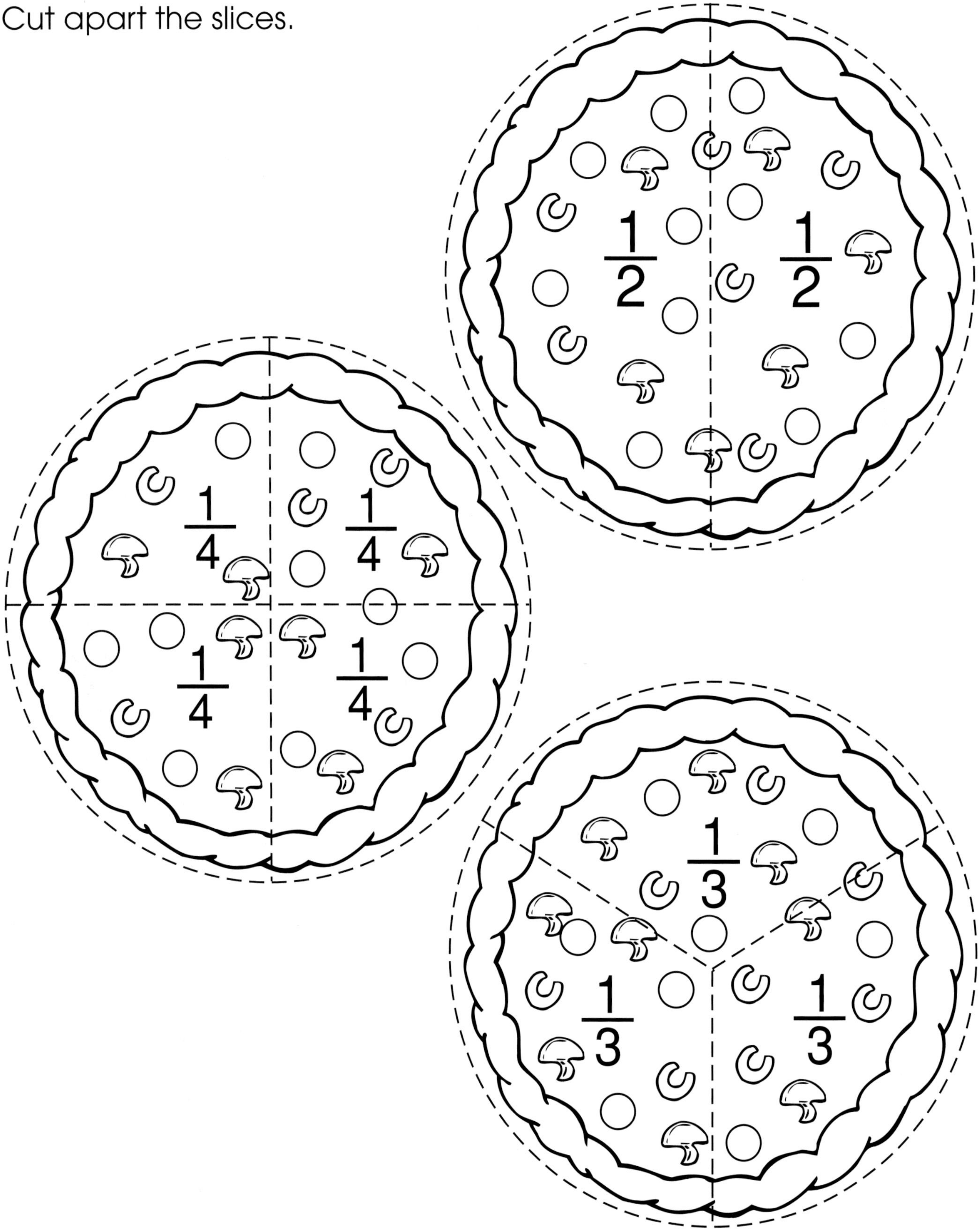

$\frac{1}{2}$ $\frac{1}{2}$

$\frac{1}{4}$ $\frac{1}{4}$

$\frac{1}{4}$ $\frac{1}{4}$

$\frac{1}{3}$

$\frac{1}{3}$ $\frac{1}{3}$

©1997 The Education Center, Inc. • Lifesaver Lessons™ • Grade 1 • TEC503

Note To Teacher: Use with "Fractions By The Slice" on page 43.

minute hand

hour hand

©1997 The Education Center, Inc. • *Lifesaver Lessons*™ • Grade 1 • TEC503

Note To Teacher: Use with "Time For A Cookie Break!" on page 51. Duplicate this page on tagboard. To assemble the clock, cut out the three pieces and use a brad to attach the two hands to the clock's face.

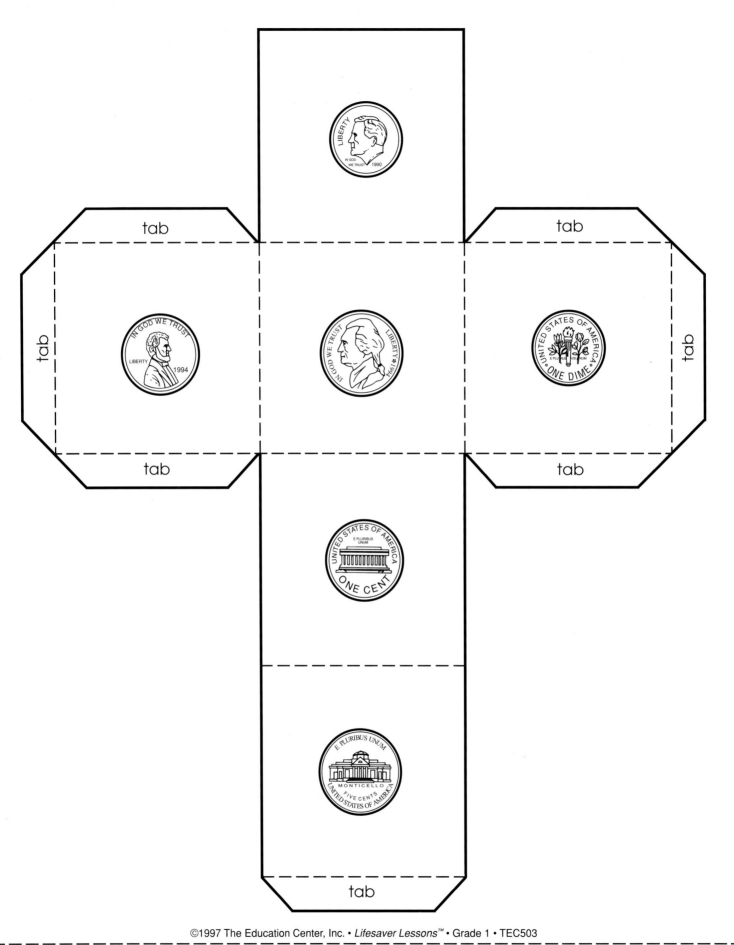

©1997 The Education Center, Inc. • *Lifesaver Lessons*™ • Grade 1 • TEC503

94 **Note To Teacher:** Use with "Ahoy, Mateys!" on page 55. To create the cube, cut along the solid line, fold along the dotted lines, and then tape together to form a cube shape.

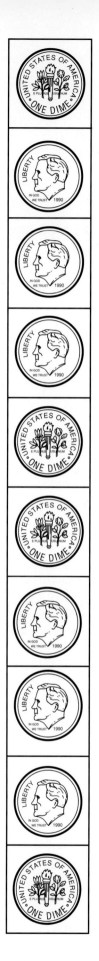

©1997 The Education Center, Inc. • *Lifesaver Lessons*™ • Grade 1 • TEC503

Note To Teacher: Use with "Ahoy, Mateys!" on page 55 and "Bakery Buys" on page 59.

Grade 1 Math Management Checklist

SKILLS	PAGES	DATE(S) USED	COMMENTS
ADDITION & SUBTRACTION			
Addition To 6	3		
Addition To 12	7		
Subtraction From 6	11		
Subtraction From 12	15		
Addition And Subtraction To 12	19		
NUMBER SENSE			
Place Value To 49	23		
Place Value To 99	27		
Sequencing Numbers To 100	31		
Ordinal Numbers	35		
Estimation	39		
Fractions: 1/2, 1/3, 1/4	43		
TIME & MONEY			
Reading A Calendar	47		
Time To Hour And Half Hour	51		
Coin Combinations To 50¢	55		
Coin Combinations To 99¢	59		
MEASUREMENT			
Nonstandard Measurement	63		
Measurement In Inches	67		
Measurement In Centimeters	71		
PROBLEM SOLVING			
Patterns	75		
Logic Problems	79		
Graphing And Tally Marks	83		
Word Problems	87		

©1997 The Education Center, Inc. • *Lifesaver Lessons*™ • Grade 1 • TEC503